AN OCTAVE
ABOVE THUNDER

BOOKS BY CAROL MUSKE

POETRY

Red Trousseau (1993)
Applause (1989)
Wyndmere (1985)
Skylight (1981)
Camouflage (1975)

NOVELS

(as Carol Muske Dukes)
Saving St. Germ (1993)
Dear Digby (1989)

ESSAYS

Women and Poetry: Truth, Autobiography
and the Shape of the Self (1997)

AN OCTAVE
ABOVE THUNDER

New and Selected Poems

Carol Muske

PENGUIN BOOKS

PENGUIN BOOKS
Published by the Penguin Group
Penguin Putnam Inc., 375 Hudson Street, New York, New York 10014, U.S.A.
Penguin Books Ltd, 27 Wrights Lane, London W8 5TZ, England
Penguin Books Australia Ltd, Ringwood, Victoria, Australia
Penguin Books Canada Ltd, 10 Alcorn Avenue, Toronto, Ontario, Canada M4V 3B2
Penguin Books (N.Z.) Ltd, 182–190 Wairau Road, Auckland 10, New Zealand

Penguin Books Ltd, Registered Offices: Harmondsworth, Middlesex, England

First published in Penguin Books 1997

1 3 5 7 9 10 8 6 4 2

Grateful acknowledgment is made for permission to reprint selections from the following publications:
    Camouflage by Carol Muske. Copyright © 1975 by Carol Muske. Reprinted by permission of the University of Pittsburgh Press.
    Skylight by Carol Muske. Copyright © 1981 by Carol Muske. Used by permission of Doubleday, a division of Bantam Doubleday Dell Publishing Group, Inc.
    Wyndmere by Carol Muske. Copyright © 1985 by Carol Muske. Reprinted by permission of the University of Pittsburgh Press.
    Applause by Carol Muske. Copyright © 1989 by Carol Muske. Reprinted by permission of the University of Pittsburgh Press.
    Red Trousseau by Carol Muske. Copyright © Carol Muske, 1993. Used by permission of Viking Penguin, a member of Penguin Putnam Inc.

Pages xi and xii constitute an extension of this copyright page.

LIBRARY OF CONGRESS CATALOGING-IN-PUBLICATION DATA
Muske, Carol, 1945–
An octave above thunder: new and selected poems/Carol Muske.
p. cm.—(Penguin poets)
ISBN 0 14 058.794 2 (pbk.)
I. Title.
PS3563.U837O28   1997
811'.54—dc21   97-10066

Printed in the United States of America
Set in Garamond No. 3
Designed by Judith Abbate

This book is dedicated to my mother and father.
And to David and Annie: my home.

ACKNOWLEDGMENTS

I would like to thank Cal Bedient and Louise Glück for their close, insightful readings of these poems in manuscript. I would also like to thank Michelle Latiolais, David St. John, and Molly Bendall for invaluable critical advice, moral support, and friendship, for which I am daily, deeply grateful.

Also, special thanks to Paul Slovak for patient editing and understanding about last-minute changes—ditto Barbara Campo! Thanks to Gerald Costanzo for unflagging support of my work —and the gift of a hardcover. And to Kim Witherspoon and Maria Massie: all my gratitude and admiration. And Susie Dubs: thanks, my Basil! My deep appreciation to Barbara Kassel, to Joe Byrne, and to Judith Hall. Thanks to Creighton University for their distinguished alumna citation. Thanks to the University of Southern California for the Phi Kappa Phi award and to Nancy Malone, O.S.U., for the "pilot" fellowship of the Association for Religion and Intellectual Life.

Some of the poems in this collection first appeared in the following periodicals:

The American Poetry Review: "Afterwards," "Blue Kashmir, '74," "Box," "Dream," "Lucifer," "Miracles," "My Sister Not Painting, 1990," "The Painter's Daughter," "Red Trousseau," "To the Muse," and "Wyndmere, Windemere"

Antaeus: "Census," "Child with Six Fingers," "Chivalry," "Fireflies," and "Skylight"

The Antioch Review: "Coral Sea, 1945," and "Monk's House, Rodmell"

The Best Verse: "Ideal"

Colorado Review: "Barra de Navidad: Envoi"

Columbia: "Blood Hour"

Esquire: "Swansong"

Field: "An Octave Above Thunder," poems 1 to 5 and 7 to 10, "August, Los Angeles, Lullaby," "Last Take" ("Unsent Letter 4,") "Prague: Two Journals (1970, 1990)," and "Worry"

The George Washington Review: "In-Flight Flick"

The Little Magazine: "Freezing to Death"

Los Angeles Magazine: "Like This"

The Missouri Review: "De-icing the Wings" and "Immunity"

Moon and Lion Tailes: Cheap Scent"

The Nation: "Pacemaker"

New England Review / Bread Loaf Quarterly: "China White" and "Ransom"

The New Yorker: "Golden Retriever," "The Invention of Cuisine," "Skid," "Summer Cold," "Surprise," and "War Crimes"

The Painted Bride Quarterly: "Hyena"

The Paris Review: "Having Fled the Cité Universitaire (Paris, 1970)"

Ploughshares: "Anna," "David," and "A Fresco"

Poetry: "Little L.A. Villanelle" and "Sounding"

Poetry Miscellany: "The Way a Swan Turns"
River Styx: "Unsent Letter 2"
The Snail's Pace Review: "Theories of Education"
Solo: "Blue Rose"
Three Penny Review: "Pediatrics"
Verse: "Ideal"
The Western Humanities Review: "At the School for the Gifted"
Woman Poet: "Special Delivery to Curtis: The Future of the World"
The Yale Review: "Field Trip"

"Benares" and the section "We Bought Amish Quilts" from "An Octave Above Thunder" appeared in *Slate*, the on-line magazine of Microsoft, Inc.

A number of the selections were reprinted in the anthologies, *The Best American Poetry 1992*, edited by Charles Simic and David Lehman (Scribner, 1992); *Mothersongs: Poems For, By and About Mothers*, edited by Sandra M. Gilbert, Susan Gubar, and Diana O'Hehir (Norton, 1995); *One Hundred Great Poems by Women: The Golden Ecco Anthology*, edited by Carolyn Kizer (Ecco, 1995); *Pushcart Prize XIII: Best of the Small Presses*, edited by Bill Henderson (Pushcart Press, 1988); and *Pushcart Prize XVIII: Best of the Small Presses*, edited by Bill Henderson (Pushcart Press, 1992).

Contents

FROM *WYNDMERE* (1985)

An Octave
Above Thunder

NEW POEMS

LIKE THIS

—*Morituri te salutamus.*
Los Angeles Times, 1927

Maybe it's not the city you thought
it was. Maybe its flaws, like cracks
in freeway pylons, got bigger, caught
your eye, like swastikas on concrete stacks.

Maybe lately the dull astrologies of End,
Millennium-edge rant about world death
make sense. Look. Messages the dead send
take time to arrive. When the parched breath

of the Owens River Valley guttered out,
real voices bled through the black & white.
The newspaper ad cried, *We who are about
to die salute you.* Unarmed, uncontrite.

Gladiators: a band of farmers, entrenched.
And how many on the Empire's side recognized
the bitter history of that bow? Greed drenches
itself in a single element, unsurprised.

Like strippers, spotlit. Tits and asses
flash red-gold, while jets shriek above.
Rim-shot. History, like a shadow, passes
over a city impervious as a bouncer's shove

to dreams. Images tell you what's imaginable.
Here comes another ton. We bathe in
what's re-routed from the source: a fable
of endless water in a dipper made of tin.

The future's in fact a few images refusing to fit
anywhere. For some: heads on pikes, sky-fires.
For others: a kid's painting of a green horse, its
bridle fallen behind. This city never seems to tire

of stupid prophecy, yet seeks no past, ways
Time talks to itself, salutes us as it dies.
We were taught to think: *like that, like this.* Days
of nights, not seeing the simile's power. It tries

to link the unlike and the like, I said aloud
to my special students, so-called troubled youth
who'd packed guns & gang caps. On campus, proud
to scare the shit out of everybody. The truth

is, they wrote *offkey,* like weird singing. So
it was quiet as one of them read his analogy:
The bullet-holes over my door, his voice low,
look like a peacock tail, a peacock fan. He

who'd never seen a shuddering strut of quills,
hadn't seen desire in that many eyes, said *I
don't think like anybody.* And why? He kills,
he's a kid. But look, he sees what we die

from not seeing—how different beauty opens
its different eyes. The expanse unfolds,
many-eyed, iridescent, it holds. Unbroken,
salutes you. The fiery gaze turns gold.

The child on the sled shields her eyes
against the moving glare of snow

looking ahead to where she's been,
growing up impatient for the precipitous

slide of thought into thought.
White fires divide: trees again.

So the landscape is never more
than an exit (the sled veering)

into beauty, not a path to person,
place, the plural surface of touch.

Red paint arrow slashed on pine,
red runners, a reflection, but no

shadow of a wolf stretching, no violin,—
just the wing of the arched board, the

child doubling the frozen rope over
her knuckles, kneeling, then lying flat

against the dropping wall of white.
Now the blue digital screen next to our

shared bed bleeds light onto newsprint:
a heap of skulls, (the sled airborne) odd

jewels flung on the mind's assessing tray.
I have no way to imagine such numb exactness

but from diminishing height, flung back into
the body on the bed where I have lain awake

all night desiring patience, desiring to read
the skull's pale calligraphy with my fingers.

So late to intercept gravity. Tender gravity,
on that windy hill meant for burial (colliding)

spikes white into cranial fire. Flame-blue
digits pause then drop: no execution, no kiss.

> . . . *reverberation*
> *Of thunder of spring over distant mountains*
> *He who was living is now dead*
> *We who were living are now dying*
> *With a little patience.*

—T. S. Eliot,
"What the Thunder Said"

1

She began as we huddled, six of us,
in the cellar, raising her voice above
those towering syllables . . .

Never mind she cried when storm candles
flickered, glass shattered upstairs.
Reciting as if on horseback,
          she whipped the meter,

trampling rhyme, reining in the reins
of the air with her left hand as she
stood, the washing machine behind her
          stunned on its haunches, not spinning.

She spun the lines around each other,
her gaze fixed. I knew she'd silenced
a cacophony of distractions in her head,
          to summon what she owned, rote-bright:

> *Of man's first disobedience,*
>   *and the fruit* . . .
> *of the flower in a crannied wall*
> *and one clear call* . . .

7

for the child who'd risen before school assemblies:
eerie Dakota rumble that rolled yet never brought
rain breaking over the podium. Her voice rose,
                              an octave above thunder:

When I consider how my light is spent—
I thought of her light, poured willy-nilly.
in this dark world and wide: half-blind, blind,
a widening distraction *Getting and spending*
we lay waste our powers . . . Different poem, a trick!

Her eyes singled me out as the wind slowed.
Then, reflective, *I'd rather be / a Pagan*
suckled in a creed outworn / than a dullard
                              with nothing by heart.

It was midsummer, Minnesota. In the sky,
the Blind Poet blew sideways, his cape spilling
rain. *They also serve!* she sang, hailing
                              closure

as I stopped hearing her. I did not want to
stand and wait. I loathed nothing so much
as the forbearance now in her voice,
                    insisting that Beauty was at hand,

but not credible. I considered
how we twisted into ourselves to live.
When the storm stopped, I sat still,
                              listening.

Here were the words of the Blind Poet—
crumpled like wash for the line, to be
dried, pressed flat. Upstairs, someone called
          my name. What sense would it ever

make to them, the unread world, the getters and spenders,
if they could not hear what I heard,
        not feel what I felt
        nothing ruined poetry, a voice revived it,
                extremity.

2

The Dakota in her speech—windy,
oddly shepherded, always bending—
lilts of Czech and Norwegian, dumb cousin Swede.

How had my task become shaking free those words
from the rhythms of her voice into the imperatives
of the poets who wrote them—

              When everything whirling otherwise
in my head re-settled syntax? From her I learned
a further thing. I heard it in her riptide parataxis:

compassion. Her wrong emphasis on the right
words shunted a way to love, the only kind I knew.

Words: off-kilter, oddly phrased and therefore
inevitable. Stumbling orphaned heart, awake at
that first funeral—who was she? Sixteen,

standing at her mother's grave. Iris, iris—
salutatorian and the smell of lilac,
                              sabotaged.

3

That spring, he told me how, as kids,
they kept teasing their poor mother
until she pointed straight up and said
Stop or you'll be struck. Then the bolt
from nowhere, lighting their stunned faces.
                                        Then thunder.

When it did strike him, years later,
he fell down alone. He'd been taunting
Mother Despair, not only in his poems.
I want him to *not stop*, to stand up again.
Years ago, he and I waded into the warm
water off Temescal. He'd shown up out of
the blue, heading south. Blond kids stood
on the lit waves. Air's undertow: love's
despair. He said, *You know what you have to do
darlin'.* We went in, no reason, laughing. No
haze: you could see all the way to the Channels.
I knew, but I didn't do it. Breakers soaked us, we
kept wading. If we'd gone on, on sheer bouyancy
like that, we'd have entered the cliche, stopping
only at the fork, where she points and it shimmers
apocalyptic: Light I've loved and refused all my life.

4

That was close they murmur, then count
off their small distance away from where
the swift electric current has seized a man
under a tree, packaging his tremors . . .

Thus Buddha, light full on his wide sly
lips, rises next to the jackal-god, shaking
her mane of singed hair: what do they care?
They are not aware of the woman shaking,

the child repeating the bad word, whirling
in place. He is a God of the senses and
he wants to fuck you. *That was close.* Inside
the mind, a spotlight. Inside the spotlight,

a voice. That's all anyone can tell you
about train schedules. The coordinates
of the shroud and the hurrying body. This
shape made by turbulence finally is a circle,

but on the horizon, where the fiery snake
swallows its tail, time collapses, distance
refuses to depart. For once it's *now*, and
this is our voice, God, simultaneous.

5

Bedda-don, bedda-don, bedda-don . . . She
chants low, all joy and menace, closing in
on the baby bit by bit. Nose to nose with
his fat worried face, she shrieks, *doots!*

and bumps his damp forehead with hers.
She's our machine, our mirror. Eyebrows up,
drawing each face into her face—the way
a thunderhead, rising, draws smaller clouds

into its brain. Kolaçe dough outgrows
the bowl. Her dizzying English speeding
through winters of immigration, wild—
night silo, night wheat: I repeat

each syllable as she speaks: *Uff-da.*
Jebroc. Dedoshek. Dream your eyes,
little mishka. In school, meaning
clings resolute to each word. Here,

brow to brow with passion's signifier
every word I've learned grows giddy,
falters. Church Latin rolls over my head,
imprinting the pale waves of frankincense.

Ad Deum qui laetificat, juventutem meam.
No rest for the wicked, she quotes, I must
have been bad! *God,* I pray, *let me live*
in my suitcase of books. Deliver me from

the green-eyed snake, the needle-arm of
the Zenith hi-fi. It winds around the bannister
at night, talks sepia to me in its jailed bass.
Dies Irae, dies illa. Tantum ergo. Throw the cow

over the fence some hay. The boy-babies bang
their skulls against the rattling crib-backs. Dawn.
Bonjour mes élèves! she calls in fractured French.
She points out the newest blossoms: peonies, lilacs,

even the ones we love just for this brief heartbeat
because they will fade in our hands, die on us,
even as we recite, in hope of resuscitation, their
actual names: *baby's breath, lily-of-the-valley, bleeding heart.*

6

We bought Amish quilts
in Kalona. Or, I bought two.
You hung back, approving,
but disinclined by nature

to purchase cotton and twill
oddments, stars and hexagons.
Yet you did. And paid with
rare optimism: a love poem.

It turns out I was the one
who did not believe. When
an ecstatic life is taken apart
then re-stitched in increments,
it comes to resemble bad faith,
a set of troubled assumptions.
My daughter sleeps under mine.

And you, who are nowhere now but
in the dark blue cloud, saw it first,
pointed out to me in love the one
bright yellow square, uncanny, unfaded
in the dim one-hundred-year-old field.

7

I once saw, just outside Santa Fe,
a horse fall to the earth on purpose.

It happened in the scene where the outlaws
came galloping across the creek, firing
their pistols into the air. The riderless
horse, galloping, knew exactly when,

as its hoof touched the far bank,
to stumble and roll on its side in
the dust—and though the cameras
blocked everything suddenly, I kept seeing it,

the sudden drop, the flailing legs. Re-lit
genesis, a fall away from God's hand. I
couldn't imagine it for a second, even as I
saw it happening, heard the impact of the body.

That morning I'd watched the wrangler
teach the horse to go down. Prompted, it
bowed, then dropped to one knee, then
the other, then slowly rolled. Deep bow,

the knee bent, head bobbing, the man showing
the horse in silence how to set the will against
instinct, how to unbalance what is built into the heart.
Each time the director nods, they come across again,

shooting, splashing as the horse begins to stagger.
Years ago you told me how an invisible river
runs through a herd of fast horses. Then
why does this animal, one of a pack trained

to act on command, push out farther than
the rest? Willing to trust a voice over its
own flowing terror, over the shots fired skyward,
the swiveling eye-sticks? I don't know if the horse

loved its trainer, if it's that easy. Easy too
to say that there was a streak beyond self-
preservation in you, some way that you calmed
yourself with your own voice as you brought yourself

to earth. But no one knows that. Your voice,
your falling to earth. That's the extent of it.
Though sometimes now I think of you as Lucifer,
whom I loved perversely as a child, listening
to my mother recite his demise. On his "faded
face" . . . "Deep scars of Thunder had intrencht"
and his heart was wild. A wild horse
still, a Lucifer, the scars came from hearing,

an octave above thunder, something splendid,
something paradisiacal, that you and only
you, in your capacity to hear and translate,
your capacity to re-make the world, would obey.

8

A winter resort in summer.
Mile high and higher.
Lupine and other obvious
flowers planted just for the poets.

Afternoon thunder. God miked,
someone said. A hawk rose
and the Wordsworthians swooned.
I was tired of the altitude,

the Duino Elegies tattooed
on everyone's ass. Sick as pitch,
I parked near the redwood slats
of the Exxon station and gunned my motor.

You got in. The whole mountain
fell into place. Believe me, I had
nothing to wish for. I still hear my
mother when I shift gears that fast.

Slow down. Somebody's heart. Emily's
Loaded Chamber. I thought I was ready to
die that July till you made me see I wouldn't.
We call it a kind of *capability:*
You just slide out of the self—then *fly*.

9

She says *Death*
and her students
scream *tombstone,*
skeleton, Grim
Reaper, hangman.

She says *Justice*
and they cry *gavel,*
courtroom, blind woman
with scales, jury.

Then one murmurs:
backyard, dirty snowdrifts,
empty coke bottle,
blind girl's plaid wool
scarf. All abstractions

translate to images,
she tells them. Then
how does the broken bottle
under the snow retrace its
strange single path of derivation?
Or this scarf, lost till the thaw?

She knows there is no way
back. A door closes. She
says *kidnapper* and suddenly

everyone sees his face.
She says *Love* and they see
nothing, they are blind.

10

Improbable, the voice of the poet:
it comes, as the Russian genius said,
from a long way off. Her tone, they
say, is untranslatable. The words are
translatable, but not the timbre
of her voice, her word-play—

not the blackness of her dawn,
her church bells, her child's fever
pealing through the Russian, resonate.
I sit at the stone gate, here by the drifting
benches of snow, just past the wind's stumbling
pursuers, the daughter's fixed gaze—

a rope over the rafter. *Heard her voice,*
may we each kneel in that swaying shadow?
Bell clapper, scythe, a military salute
unimaginable at the empty well. Let us
praise *a long way off,* the long shadows
in a poet's voice. Each line, she said
(up over the rafter)—translated,

was *intonation.* Then, silence.
(The line taut.) Then what we still
gather, like wolves, from the swaying
distance, improbable, untranslatable:

Exile, lilac, dichtung, lucifer,
bonjour, sushchnost, blood
stumbling in the heart: its dazzling

repetitive *once*, like thunder.

Having Fled the Cité Universitaire

(Paris, 1970)

I rented an atelier attached to the flat
of a fading French film star, Marie-Claire—
who sighed, shaking out her trademark titian hair,
then rolled a joint, lit up the dollar/franc debate.

I was made to feel, for the first time in my life,
like an American. It was a past I'd planned to lose
and *fast;* yet the Yank accent, blond hair to my butt,
tie-dyed Levis, were what landed me (by luck?) in *Hair,*

on a strobe-lit, hyper-choreographed self-dare.
An "Auditions" sign on Boul' St. Denis had drawn me.
Summoned down center, at Théâtre Porte St. Martin, shocked
at my sudden, weird élan, I belted "Easy to Be Hard."

(The callback, a blue pneu, came with producer's card.)
The French cast was cruel, the only time I stripped for
the nude scene they "disappeared" my jeans, my "pull-ovair."
Curtain-wrapped, I hissed, *filthy frogs! ici la guerre!*

Still, the troupe's lovely star praised me, took me
post-show, to eat escargots at Les Halles. At dawn,
delivery trucks honked, then backed up, burying her car
under bushels of parsley: avalanche of green snow.

Inside, as wipers parted the grassy sea, she kissed me.
Confused, I wrote poems in the wings till the house-
lights flickered. At the first chords of "Aquarius,"
I crouched, then tom-tom'd onstage—every inch

our director's Rousseau-red notion of a girl-brave.
Back at Marie-Claire's, a terrible artist (now dead)
had stacked his bad paintings near my bed: they bled
into my dreams. When the old concierge cackled and

called me Petite Malheureuse, she meant I was too
inept to trip the *minuterie* on each landing
before the bulb below blinked out: I climbed blind.
Late afternoons, I sipped hash tea with Marie-Claire,

then set off for the theater *seule,* thinking how odd
it was I'd come all the way across the sea to under-
study the role of a bimbo in love with a Hell's Angel.
Yet I knew just enough about poetry to take notes from

the chorus: knowing one night I'd step into that lit spot
transfigured, star-hot. Baring only my soul, shaking out
my trademark hair, I'd speak my lines in a new voice,
like Marie-Claire: before all of Paris, I would sing.

MIRACLES

for Charles Simic

Think about it:
                    The siren finds its migraine, the fix its junkie,
the bomb flowers up under the foot of the Goodwill Ambassador
                              as he turns the ignition key . . .

Miracles, nothing but miracles!
                         I heard the faith healer
complain about his arthritis to his wife, a dwarf, stone deaf.

          Hallejuah! The one person on earth to whom he could
convey his great pain can't hear him. Neither can he, who
lays hands on the afflicted, rolling back his eyes,
                              lengthen her bones one notch.

Stasis and apocalypse, stasis and apocalypse. The stopped wind
and the wind of destruction together deface the spotlit virgin
               and the Good Humor Man shooting up at her feet.

What more can we ask of the miraculous?
When the Holy Ghost appears to a bulldog
(himself a lifelong skeptic), the house catches fire—
the bulldog barks but cannot rouse his master, facedown
                              on the couch.

O the night is so bright, so filled with possibility!
The hammer finds the thumb, the gas leak the flame—

the long-winded poet, hunched over the podium,
struck by a falling EXIT sign

is proof, I tell you! Miracles—
nothing but miracles.

L.A. spring, our boulevard of flowering jaca-
randa. Twelve trees: Ophelia's delirium. The
color the clapper makes inside the bell, the bell's
explosion twelve times into addled violet. I see

the equal signs, but no two things on this
earth are the same. The symbol of wings that
follows me is the real maker of equations:
blue rain and my dogs panting beside me.

See. That's my dark Expressionist painting the first
extraneous cross: dying Christ as just an element of
landscape, like *blue:* the hare's throat, the contusion
of clouds, backlit, and the varying mountain sky. Count

the intrusion of a dog's bark. Trout-fishing in Kashmir,
I followed my guide faithfully, a child into white water.
He pointed deep, deeper into the Himalayas. *There*
was China. Dressed as a boy, I didn't know how to paint

my own naivete: everything in my gaze faithful, true as a dog's.
August 15th. Lower Wangat. Below us the Jhelum was flooding
into Srinigar. Consequences, dark as blood mixed with cerulean,
the color in the skull as the head dips underwater. The beggar's

"long gone" cry like the floating arias of the peddlers, little boat-
sleighs criss-crossing Dal Lake, loaded with gold and bones stolen
from Tibetan temples. The hotel-houseboats capsized, but not
every one. Woe is the woman who walks in blue, it's her ecstasy

she cannot see it. At the Oberoi, the Hindu Female
Doctor I'd placed in the book of strong women pulled me aside,
veiled, hissing. *They will kill me.* I stepped into the whitewater.
The dogs look back at me, race the wave-colored hill. She un-

dressed the Moslem women, which was forbidden. Eyes turned
sideways above the veil, then a downward glance. She saw that
they required the cautery blade, biopsy. He pointed out a trout.
Dun-flash. She had to find the soft places where the tumors hid,

behind breastbone or ovary. On the wall, sunlight:
her bone chart, twenty blue vials of penicillin.
She was the first unsteady step into the secular,
into expression. An element in the landscape: rain

pencilling itself on the glass as they stepped free
of their veils, naked: breasts, buttocks. The neigh-
bor's bucket seats overflow with blue wings, the trees'
sex. The women stood, ecstatic, keeping their arms

straight, perpendicular to the floor. Equal sign,
I don't know how anyone could change sex so ex-
peditiously. I wore jeans, my hair under a cap.
He must have opted to look the other way, away

from the waves. The men accosted her in the street,
shouted how she'd defiled their wives. *Help me.*
Her eyes. He taught me how to thread on the fly, cast.
The tree holds out its arms: falling blossoms.

I begged off. Eyes, eyes, the color of the dogs', crosses.

We floated on that skiff at day-
break. Down the Ganges to the ghats.
The joyful dead bumped against
the bow, their faces attentive.

Now that I understand the similar
nature of our claims, I realize
what they were trying to tell us.
I am not a woman of the law, but

a dumb lover of shapes. That's the
way the river works, spinning its
strong lines, a rapt circle into which
the dead can fit. I watched you standing

near the smoking black cribs, your arms
wrapped round yourself, set in your own
embrace. The ones who burned became wings
lifting into dawn. The ones who chanted

became eyes. Then the bearded holy man appeared,
walking through flames, straight to me, pressing
my brow with his dirty thumb. *Baksheesh!*
he cried, smearing the single red dot: sunrise.

Yes, I wanted them to levitate.
Unfortunately, I hadn't a leg to stand on.
Cut-out camels plodded across the blackboard's high
sill. Yet the desert below refused to unfurl its
mica wings. When I asked them to try to remember,
to release a soap bubble from their marvelous arsenal

of wands, they resisted. They lined up, suspicious
in individual spotlights. The fountain inside
the scissored palm could only rise so high,
maybe just a trumpeted C. Which is high, but
not like those huge blue dreams that used to float by,
shot from cloud-atomizers, the original public breeze

on its back in the grass. Let's try to guess who
or what is being borne up by this caravan of thin-
skinned humps, a-bulge, inoculated? I tell you
every one has a rider, a crop. It's been done
this way for some time. If we pause here by the pillars
of sand, up to our poet-knees in anarchy, won't each

gulp of hoarded water from the toppled monument be
sweeter passed hand to hand in the sun-colored dipper?
Up to our thighs in it now, and spared what drills it-
self into the rock daily, so it can claim to know zero
after zero, and make that nothing into a sound like
silent bells, split parched hooves, plodding.

Fist pounding in a mitt, a kid
sits, furious, across from us. He
doesn't want to cool his heels like
this. He'd rather bounce a few off

the sighing doors that shut us out.
Inside, a live wire probes your heart.
Probes the top lobe, then underneath,
the bloodless, gunned one—the one

fitful as neon spitting in a glass
wrist. I've brought you a paper cone
of roses, plus this other implacable kid:
the one they never let step up to bat.

Your sons hunched in the dugout, razzed
and spat. Even behind your back, they
wouldn't mock those right-of-Goldwater
ticked-off soliloquies. But I would step

up, unbidden. Smart off into a wide
swing: intercepting the pitch meant
for a player. Imagine my right line drive
past the diamond's horizon, my cake-walk

gaudy saunter to third! I can't stop
replaying that. I slump now with my bouquet,
lulled by the hiss of pneumatic ins and outs.
Stung by a wire sunk wrist to *it,* the heart

trips back into self-imitation. Roses:
a dugout, cries, and the petals echoing each
other, bound by wire. The mad kid slides the
whole length of the waiting-room tiles,

steals home.

Blossoming white in the rose garden,
Plucked at dusk by my daughter's hand:
Colorless rose, it's fate you resemble.

When the young sorceress leans
Over the glass bowl where you float,
Staining the surface with her shadow,

Three dye-drops from a kitchen vial:
She believes she re-invents you.
Hers is the passion of the alchemist,

All matter burns before her in that
Pale reconstructive fire. See how she
Clutches the vial to her new breasts?

She desires a sky-colored rose. I
Hear you gasp, drawing the tincture
Up through your veins till each petal

Is blue-tinged, bruised as an eyelid.
Legends warned of your poison blood,
The thorn-prick, deep amniotic sleep.

In this version, harm spirals dark
Up the stem, exacting perfection. *White
Blossoms.* What is this life, corrected

To a dreamed-of shade? Like you,
She is innocent. She floats there,
My vial emptied, running in her veins.

FROM *CAMOUFLAGE* (1975)

It was too big to take on the subway
so she came to it every day
that winter in the room
where it waited on one foot,
sly seabird.

She sat down and opened her hands,
parted the wings one by one
till it flew ahead of her fingers
singing
the lame foot skidding on gold.

The sun turned its back on the glass
and paled as she sat
obstinate
green-eyed
her foot on its foot
pumping.

The fire died.
Snow hissing at the window.
Above her head a baroque hailstorm
failed in 4/4 time. She sang,
unable to hold the bright hinge
to her heart.
Lame savior she sang.
It bowed as she left
and sat, chastened by scales,
wondering.

The late Miss H. came to us Wednesdays at four
direct from the steno pool.
We waited, twenty of us in toe shoes,
slumped against her basement barre.

She was big,
her white hair bobbed,
her blue fox insurance against
ladies who called her déclassé.

Sometimes she told us how it was
when she danced *Les Sylphides*—
she, the ingénue with natural turnout,
withers drawn in the white light
of favored nations.
The Bolshoi sent its guns for her,
the heavy breathers from Minsk.
Miss H. leaped through their lines unruffled,
the season at her feet.
(Her lover Hans, a simple huntsman,
was at her side
the night in Dubrovnik
when a cab crushed her great toe.)

The swan died officially in St. Louis in '53
on a makeshift stage strewn with roses.
She gave her all,
then came to St. Paul
where she taught us "toe dance."

She often wept, sipping brandy,
nodding when the needle stuck
on a crack in *Romeo and Juliet*.
Those days we stood on ceremony.
Mute sisters of the dance, we froze
holding second position till six
when the mothers came.

1

The bedclothes grow stiff around my body.
The pitcher cracks. Light comes,
losing heat. I sit blowing ghosts into my wrists
nursing old skepticism.

Getting out of bed
I step into a drift.
It is falling everywhere now—
into my shoes, the vases,
the baskets of painted cherries.

2

My body moves bladelike through mirrors.
My head turns, a spool winding down
the last great ring of bone at the throat.
Cape of quartz. It snaps
light along the spaces of my spine,
pressing speechless against the marrow—
dead thumbs on a buzzer.

3

Who breaks my little imprints into salt?
Sparrow tracks. A new brightness
rises in my lungs.

When I open my mouth
it comes out in a stream.
Skinless. Circuit of stars.

4

I've scratched a message on an icicle.
My palm rests on the table,
a snowstorm in progress beneath it.
My thumbs itch.
My left heel burns.
They say you don't feel a thing.

I felt no pain when they cut it off
only a coldness like rain
on the edge of the hand
where it was
the ache came later

it grew crooked
its sense was different, sixth
a feel for passing shapes
edges, lips of bells or bark

sometimes I tied it with string
it sang to the thumb

I lean on trees now
feel the roughness with my shoulders
they gave me a ball
instead I watch birds fly
thinking of wings

SALAD DAYS: NEBRASKA, 1964

for John T.

1

On the plane
that doubled as crop duster,
hunching with the drunken pilot,
I watched the land
run jackrabbit
for miles,
ragged as our own small flight
from the dull imperative of sky.

Under us rolled
the casual gravity of Nebraska
sulking in our shadow,
sucking in its bitten lip of cloud.
Me and the '64 flight-school ace
heading downwind in a Cessna.

Out on the airstrip
signals ignite,
the feedbag full of butterflies
explodes in the opposite direction.
The tower woos us with radar
but we slip under its net,
turn due west to the panhandle,
and bend to the landscape,
pollen dropping from the wings.
Our target: summer, its unidentified harvest
blowing gold dust through the loam.

Out there, twenty thousand acres
roll back and draw our fire:
he tips the joystick—
we dive.

2

the angel drinking gin rickeys
alone on the drafty dance-floor
ruining her one silk dress
in the dark
I called Janie
as I came to claim her
in time for curfew

so late we were skating back
over the ice of the campus path
truant
her head against mine
against the sad platinum moon
the sure shine of her broad teeth
as she kissed me
and called me Tommy
her ginbreath a pale blossom in the cold

a rose
she pinned to the white wings of her hair
in the wind
cracking her patent-leather flats
in the rough spots
she rubbed with vaseline

the angel humming cha cha cha
through the unprecedented snowfall
of that year

she flew through the windshield
and they plowed the water-marked silk
and the blonde hair
under the rich soil
for good

on Saturdays
I waited there where the angel lay
thinking how much they hated us

3

John T., the doctor's son, loved horses.
A photograph taken at Ames shows us
neck and neck
John T., me and the state fair stallion,
all of us
light-eyed, exhausted,
our breathing paced
to dreams of the grandstand,
the horseshoe of roses
dropped from heaven.

He was a thoroughbred,
full of a patient, irregular grace,
his neck held taut,
cheekbones faintly marked.
In the pale grass
his green eyes fired us
like ribbons he'd won
slumming in suburban derbys—
not steeplechase—
but barrel jumps and
dead man's canter.

He rode Pocoroncho
though his own nightmares,
riding heat to its center,
its dead heart lessened
by other pumping.

To stay the dreams of doctors
he rode away defiant—
failing at last in the homestretch
his eyes flying to mine,
but my eyes were already hooves,
the hooves running on blood.

4

All spring that year
the storm of copper lilacs
imprisoned by screens
rubbed against each other
voiceless, discontent,
their plaintive smell
laying siege to my senses
as I sat under the orange lamp
reading Byron.

Taking fond stock of my melancholy:
this one dead, a hero—
that one, lying to me
night after night
on the princess phone,
a sweet wind through the screen
smelling of war and treachery . . .

How the lilacs waved that spring,
purple cohorts
and the wolf prepared to come down slowly
on an old suspicious fold.

*Those things which are most evident
of all are to the intellect what the
sun is to the eye of an owl.*

—Aquinas

5

To prove God
is to deny him.
His quiddity a desperate scent
like the smell
the fox gives off,
cornered.

There is the pale argument of the afternoon
dying slightly on our hands.
To prove God
requires Aquinas and desire,
a failed momentum.

The window draws long spokes of sun
to its hub.
Ten thousand miles away
a man of God is consumed by fire,
flaming judgment of our penchant
for proof,
the iron logic of the curse:
to plead again and again
our argument,
turning the land to fiery
answers.

This year begins
the slow descent to Hell,
the Asian war,
the ghost crusade

and John T.
nodding at his desk
moves idle to a loss
more final than exile.
This war will claim him
waking, late
his eyes hold sun like syllogism.

To prove God
you must *be* him,
young and untried
stumbling drunk through the twilight wheat
roaring to a new failed moon
your prophecy
your life.

6

What it means to be a mutant,
to force the cruelest truce to blossom;
that failed landscape exacting, at last,
compassion.

For a while we lay down
on the quick-moving earth.
It took us
untied like violet along the sunken river
at sunset

to where our own eyes
could find a little peace:
some green hem of the river,
unclean
but breathing.
The summer dusk instructive:
John T. and the angel,
their bodies, their eyes
final as desire.
And the sun for once incorruptible,
at pains to spare them waste—
God or winter,
the pale reaped season impending.

Those salad days, those dusks,
when crops rose shoulder-high
and waited
green
deceived
for harvest.

She finds grief, her meat,
on a plateau
full of the moon's ammunition.
Her cousins follow, lift eyes
wide as torches
in the storm rock.
Dream birds lengthen
like wounds in the sky.

The shadow's task is primitive:
to sense doom and follow it.
She comes each distance to death
and eats what light is left.

It is her laughter on the slopes
at night.

FROM *SKYLIGHT*
(1981)

It's a kind of blindness.
I'm too familiar with the style,
the images that mark his middle period.
Driving home: the road takes on
his shapes (the eyes, the cruciform fires) . . .
Always the same grove of trees
keeping his *Black Picnic*:
people eating in rows
with bones underfoot.
Could they know the brush
that drew sparks on every surface,
that picked them out like familiar stars in the dark?

Never mind the white lies,
I know the murder in a painter's eye
as he reaches for red.
I was the child sent to bed in a prism,
the triangular room under the roof
where a spider blew threads
then walked the visible second of breath.
I saw the sun flattened by his hand,
the clouds stacked like acrobats—
at six my little house of sticks hit by lightning:
one bold stroke, the lash against canvas
alight with my privacy. I watched him come over the hill
lugging thunder in a black case.

I watched him nail a vein for the red river
in *Borneo*,
lift my face for the face of the midget in *Quint*,

stick that fifth-of-an-inch grin of his own
on *Fool's Moon*.
Where it stays to trail me.

He began by assembling clues:
the glass, the telephone and blue soap.
Coaxing the murder that no one saw
from the stubborn evidence of light.

The ventriloquism of color, he said.
Purple and green bleeding through white.
The plum split in the skeleton's hand.
See through the suspension, he said
and I see snow fences, the red skull of sun.
Driving west
the windshield a question of light fielded
left.
Speeding, I see all
he chose for me to see.

Please. Imagine the two of us
out walking in a stubbled field at sunset
watching a fox rise and turn for the woods.
Imagine my cries—for the fox
run down like this to his life.
Knowing how next to me
the fox runs in his eyes
and dies
in a typical nimbus of light.
Imagine my cries in the center of that sight.

Though it appears we are carefree,
in the photograph we look sleepy—

just like any father and daughter
out watching the sun go down.

Imagine for a moment
the still life of our meals,
meat followed by yellow cheese,
grapes pale against the blue armor of fish.

Imagine a thin woman
before bread was invented,
playing a harp of wheat in the field.
There is a stone, and behind her
the bones of the last killed,
the black bird on her shoulder
that a century later
will fly with trained and murderous intent.

They are not very hungry
because cuisine has not yet been invented.
Nor has falconry,
nor the science of imagination.

All they have is the pure impulse to eat,
which is not enough to keep them alive
and this little moment
before the woman redeems
the sprouted seeds at her feet
and gathers the olives falling from the trees
for her recipes.

Imagine. Out in the fields
this very moment
they are rolling the apples to press,
the lamb turns in a regular aura of smoke.

See, the woman looks once behind her
before picking up the stone,
looks back once at the beasts,
the trees,
that sky
above the white stream
where small creatures live and die
looking upon each other
as food.

Coral Sea, 1945

—*for my mother*

My mother is walking down a path
to the beach.
She has loosened her robe,
a blood-colored peignoir,
her belly freed
from the soft restraint of silk.
In a week I will be born.

Out on a reef
a small fleet waits for the end of the world.
My mother is not afraid.
She stares at the ships,
the lifting mask of coral,
and thinks: *the world is ending.*
The sea still orchid-colored before her
and to the south the ships in their same formation

but now the reef extends itself,
the sea thrusts up its odd red branches
each bearing a skeletal blossom.
I have no desire to be born.

In the coral sea
the parrots sing in their bamboo cages
the pearls string themselves in the mouths of oysters
it snows inside the volcano

but no one believes these things.

And these things are not believable:
not the reef feeding itself
nor the ships moving suddenly, in formation.

Nor my body burning inside hers
in the coral sea
near the reef of her lungs

where I hung in the month of December.
In the year the war ended
the world opened,
ending for me
with each slow tremor
cold
invisible as snow
falling
inside the volcano.

This is a poem of ransom
for the child walking,
her white shoes and sash
growing whiter in the dark

the stars growing white above her.
Stolen by her parents
away from the park
and the safe streets . . .

The child is walking in the dark,
dreaming the baby back in the carriage,
back in the arms of the nurse
and further back

she is dreaming the arms of the star,
the blue poppy. There are carp in the pools.
There are fools everywhere
with parasols and white canes

and she is walking through the dark
with a gun to her head,
through miles of white blindfold.
The car is humming next to the curb,

they are calling her
but she keeps walking. The night is being built
by the architect of darkness in just this way,
exact in every detail to the night she was born . . .

And what does she see, walking?
The dead in the graveyards demanding their elegies,
the blood of the first son on the doorstep,
stars levying tax for their bright insufficiency.

She is saving each white coin of thought
for blood money, for a poem of walking
away, years later, from the man and woman in her mind,
who sit at the kitchen table.

Her shoes are pure white now.
She will keep walking,
the car will stop following, the graveyard
will yield up its few tarnished words

and the poem will begin, years later
the ransom note written.
She knows this for certain:
she will have herself back.

She was the one who put her tongue
to the whetstone on its rickety wheel
in the Tool Room. The wheel spun,
the tongue arched in its bud and bent

against that dizzy syllable of grit.
Still she could never say what she meant.
When she had her tenth birthday cake
that winter, she stuttered her thanks for

the new blades, skated backward on the rink
into a room holding the sunset. The snow was falling
in it, unstoppered, odorless as chloroform.
Under the x'ed surface of the ice hung

a gold tuft from the day her brother flooded
and made the retriever sit in the wet as it
hardened. He was a pup then, but was trained to obey.
It made him mean, doing what anyone said to do,

but he did it all the same. Down in the rec
room, she pushed 12 on the Rock-Ola and the
records wobbled on their neon stalk, the red
planets circled each other inside the glass.

It was a room for fun, they said, and though
it was, it still lit up with loss, the kind that
comes from debts collected. Or so she imagined—
piano and pool table: odd courtesies of foreclosure.

On the polished bar a lit triptych said *Hamm's Beer*, its waterfall of blue tinsel rippling behind the beaver paddling a canoe up front. *The retriever, trained to hunt, would point for minutes at a dying*

bird, then fetch whatever you sent him for—till he bit a neighbor's child who touched his unhealed sore. What happened happened. No cause and effect connected her tongue and her troubled heart and never would. The pain

came on its own and pointed for minutes at whatever was wounded before her. In the end, she might have to break its neck, because of that pain. Maybe she imagined a family on the edge of a windy precipice

and—just like that, retrieved them as she stood at the opened door of the jukebox, sliding in a few new disks for her dad. Maybe she could bring back his hand on her shoulder as they stood staring into the glass

juke singing "Rock Island Line." *A bird hurt bad will wing-limp for acres to save itself.* She knew even then it was better to be dead than weaponed in her way and laid down like a ragged prize at the foot of his dream, his least sufficiency.

WORRY

for Sister Jeanne d'Arc

For some of us, they're the same,
memory and worry. At six, obsessed
with the bough that breaks in the lullaby,
I stayed awake, thinking about a cradle's
wingspan. I took the first lilacs to school

that year in a kind of gauze bunting, expecting
their necks to snap before I had them in
the hands of the nun I still call John Dark.
She turned from a window where I often stood

sill-high, afraid to look over the ledge.
On the wall, Christ stood on his cross
like a man lashed to a kite. I had been
taught to believe he would hold us all up—

spreading his arms like wings across
the cracked lilies of plaster, spreading
his arms like a florist I once saw stripping
the innocent boughs for blossoms to stick
in chicken wire. *If they take your flowers,*

they might call you sweetheart, they might
catch you up with your sad bouquet and whirl
you round and round too close to the window
for comfort. Don't forget it was springtime,

when even nuns get crazy. Don't forget
though it felt like heaven on earth,
we were on the third floor.

Poem

There is a world
made entirely of paper,
and when I think
of the little tree of my brain
on its stem

I know what feeds the conflagration.
The sun is uncivilized
and thank god for that.
These debates between the just
and the hungry don't make sense of this:

the percussion of snow,
the bloody cymbals.

But take the bible,
take all the books,
and here is a summary:

the stutter of life on these keys,
the brain's shrub red to the thorns
with thought. In that final hour,
we will stand on our words
for proximity to heaven

and the soul will sit patient
on its stair, telling its
indecipherable alphabet.

FIREFLIES

for Edward Healton

We walked together up that country road.
It was dark. Vermont. Another season.
Then, looking up, we saw the sky explode
with fireflies. Thousands, in one frisson
of cold light, scattered in the trees, ablink
in odd synchrony. That urgency,
that lightning pulse, would make us stop, think
of our own lives. The emergency

that brought us here. The city, separation
and the pain between us. Your hands that heal
can't make us whole again; this nation
of lovestruck bugs can't change that. Still, we feel
the world briefly luminous, the old spark
of nature's love. Around us now, the dark.

CHIVALRY

In Benares
the holiest city on earth
I saw an old man
toiling up the stone steps
to the ghat
his dead wife in his arms
shrunken to the size
of a child—
lashed to a stretcher.

The sky filled with crows.
He held her up for a moment
then placed her
in the flames.

In my time on earth
I have seen few acts of true chivalry,
man's reverence
for woman.

But the memory of him
with her
in the cradle of his arms
placing her just so in the fire
so she would burn faster
so the kindling of the stretcher
would catch—

is enough for me now,
will suffice
for what remains on this earth
a gesture of bereavement
in the familiar carnage of love.

Garters lying like pale insects
on her thighs
and jazz, ephemeral, familiar,
roses floating in a bowl.
The moment fills with birds
and she becomes sure of the music
as a habit of plumage,
a silk dress she wears to death.

She lets him cross a carpet,
lets him touch her face

and later
a lake:
indistinct dancing.

And later,
shaking out her hair,
she touches the soft trammeled planet
of the atomizer, blowing cheap scent
in the air
                    where it remains
like an excessive gesture. He says
she appears blind from the side,
a white craving presses against her profile.
White Shoulders. Toujours Moi.

She walks all the way back,
rain drowns in a gutter

falling down to the lake
far below her shoes.

A garter in her mind
presses hard against a metal chair,
a bare leg,
and lingers there

as tenderness,
unmentionable pain.

After a while
in weariness
the body would relinquish
some of its gifts of ingratiation:

the power of muscle to rise slightly above bone
the power to arch the pelvis as in sex
the ability of hands to press air
in gestures of supplication
or tenderness.

And in this reduction,
the body, inevitably,
would grow softer,
more attached to its surroundings,

the eyes taking in the room
its pageant of bad taste
the important masks of the torturers.

And the brain in the body
would imagine the emptiness of this room
in ten years
the intent of wilderness within it,
of rubble,
the rose growing through the grilled transom
above the doorway—

and would feel such pity
and so apart from other men in this sentiment—

that the great nerve
which runs from head to pelvis
which makes us courteous
shy
scrupulous
makes us touch one another with gentleness

would tremble
till it was plucked
held in the pliers
then in the fire

shriveling in that little violence
of heat and light

which in another form
we often refer to
as love.

CENSUS

Here's how we were counted:
firstborn, nay-sayers,
veterans, slow-payers,
seditionists, convicts,
half-breeds, has-beens,
the nearly defined dead,'
all the disenfranchised live.

Once everybody had a place
among the nameless. Now we
can't afford to be anonymous.

Consider, they said, the poor,
the misfit—consider the woman
figuring herself per cent.

Consider the P.A. system making
a point so intimate I petition
not to be anybody's good guess
or estimate. I ask to be one:

maybe widow-to-be watching the sun
diminish brick by brick along the jail
wall and also that green pear
on its drunken roll out
of the executioner's lunch basket.
At 12:01, 02, in the cocked chamber
of the digital clock
the newsman said: *There'll be less
work in the new century.* And my job

will be, as usual, forgetting—
or getting it backwards—

each non-integer, tender and separate,
fake rosebud, Rolodex, cab full of amputees
obedient to traffic, moss on the baby's headstone . . .

minus and minus' shock each minute,
the kiss, its loss,
each newborn and condemned-to-be
in one breath executed, and blessed.

Take my best friend up to your rooms,
show her the painting, the woman's face
laughing at nothing but the tattoo
of a heart on a part of the body we hide.

Show her the books, the way
scent unwinds from the syllable
of incense. But save till last
the place that came to me

afterward so often in my dreams—
the steps leading up,
then ending in sky.
And in dreams, for nights at a time,

I would imagine finding a few stars
I could stand on, facing north
into the world of the poor.
Let her see the view last,

the sky light, so that she can imagine
architecture,
a literature that dissolves into air. I
know the world is full of hopeful people,

the obliging poor of your world tour,
who listened to you
standing in sun in their tired skins,
with their friends, their little property.

But what would the government do
with a world this familiar?
Where would the empire extend itself
if the poor forfeited their longings?

The greenhouse reels in its glass capacity,
the flora inside diminished in fact.
Ex-friend, there's an elevator
that never stops rising,

there's a house hung in the sky
where you sit with my best friend,
my umbrella full of holes.
Everyday now I go into my life

where, often, it's raining
and the night's as small as a pair of hands.
I have found comfort lately
in the notion of gravity,

how the bread stays on the blue plate.
How my best friend places weight on one foot,
                                        walking.

All that is the gift of limit

beyond it is the scaffold of passion
beyond it is the sky—
to which I had right
all that time.

The sky over Cyprus is blue and usual. And you want me to move there for politics. Believe me, the sky over Manhattan is white. Everyday the same parade passes on Fifth Avenue.

And even if we could demonstrate, join hands as far downtown as that last bar, our lives would not try convention.

What women we are! One drink and the radio's topical nonsense makes sense, the way destiny appeals to the hopeless. That's politics.

And I take no pride in circumstance. There's an ambitious biography writing itself in my future having to do with the dirty white proscenium of the park and the occasion it frames: two women, a traffic light stuck on red.

I'm a feminist. There are the lives we need to survive and those we don't. Of course, everyone loves a crippled debutante. Everyone loves a calendar. Did you say it was Wednesday? *I'm a feminist.* Don't take that chair, we're expecting a feminist. Is there life after rhetoric?

No. Just this moment. Two women. The future of the world. And this poor light holding the only crown it owns over your incomparable profile, the brilliant manifesto of your hair.

FROM *WYNDMERE*
(1985)

Blood Hour

The long grass blows flat
as I pass through it, dreaming,
with my taller brother and the .22.
He is teaching me how to handle a rifle.

Early sunset rakes across our path:
three burning clouds, the great
chieftains, rise above us.

When I look through the sight
I see the door opening miles away
across the plains, a woman setting
an old cradle out on her porch.

My brother puts his arm around
my shoulders from behind, his head
cocked next to mine—adjusting
the arm's cantilever, adjusting
as much as he can, the crooked line of fire

that I will see, in reverse,
from the next second forward:
from the cradle to the burning island
on which we stand—
from the dead bullet to the barrel
and back into the live shell chamber.

Weep, for the world's wrong.

—*Dirge*, Shelley

The washed dresses stood on thin air.
You plucked them with distracted grace.
A wind-mother, a plane appearing
between the sun and me, its wings spread

in a stunned arc where the still mind
trails in bright windows of vertigo:
you held me close, you let me go.

We sat on the back step and read
together. Not like two, but one
being split apart by some shadow-
butcher. I could feel that violence

shudder under my nails, looked away
from the page, as if the backyard,
the blue stalks of rhubarb, the red
swing, could stop the invisible

passage of one being through another,
the march of infant clothes
on the line, beheaded.
You said, "I'm a tough farm girl

from Wyndmere, nothing fazes me."
Nothing fazed me either, I said.
You drew your town in the dust,
then the thin spires of wind

that grew so tall they split
us up. Now, on a plane, I fly
beside myself. I read
because you said to. The years

pull, dazed as a line of print,
afloat in the life jacket of prose.
Poetry's the air we drown in together,
mother. Poetry's the turning room,

the clear field mined with words
you read first. In Wyndmere, you said,
federal men waited by the dry well
with a paper, with justice

that could turn you outlaw.
In the wind, on the back step,
you spoke the words of poets
who got it right again and again,

in a world so wrong,
it measures only loss
in those crosses of thin air.
In the blowdown and ascent

of the separator, the mother,
whose face catches once,
then turns from me, again and again.

in purposeful white speed,
the way the Best Man, drunk,
doffs his hat to the swan . . .

Like lovers in a duel of intuition
they drift and burn, standing apart.
As if he'd never knelt in the darkness,

calling, as if she'd never risen,
shattering the clear surface
to eat slowly from his hand.

The wind sculpts itself into distance,
the drunk bows, the swan glides away
under the trees bent with age,

beneath the lifted swords of the statues.
I turn away from the window in my white dress
to the hinged mirror where

I become a procession of brides.
My mother stands, fastening
lace to lace—her hand

moving so fast it exceeds
gesture. *You don't let people love you.*
Let the mirror scatter its affections,

let me lift my glass, let him stand by my side,
with the others, one by one, let them love me
as I loved the sun igniting the veil

as we walk in the park after the ceremony.
Enigmatic as a bride, she turns to me,
twisting the ring on her finger, veiling

her face in the purest lack of emphasis,
in the face of love's fiercest commandment:
let them touch you

Look how the swan turns and turns in the blue pond.
The sky fills with invisible comets.
The carousel flings itself round a painted center

from which the wooden horses shy,
lifting their hooves, their torn eyes,
to the mechanized ceiling

where the gears raise
and lower them like skulls
on pikes, like her face

turning away from mine
in rapt sequence: mirror,
snowfall, swan, mother,

one little love after another.

CHINA WHITE

—M.S.H.

Lately your eyes watch me
out of animal eyes,
out of the sad clerk's eyes
at the makeup counter.
She didn't have the right shade
of shadow, but I charged to my account
the kind of green I chide myself with.

I kept thinking—
Why did you take so long to cry?
You were just fifteen
when it happened.
Still, you insisted on indifference,
like the Stoics, you said.

Next day, in class, leaves fell
from your Latin book.
He had gloves on, you said later,
when I held you, in that strange room
where you finally wept.
There were leaves beneath,
I couldn't breathe.

As usual, I got you laughing—
we made up our eyes,
you disembodied your gaze
with China White and gray.

You didn't cry again.
That night you sang the Magnificat
for Glee. It wasn't in your voice

to rephrase the virgin's words
but there's a part where she accepts it,
accepts the miracle they want her body for

and your eyes came looking for mine
as you sang, moving slowly at first,
then faster: face to face to face.

Too hot to sleep,
she watches the night
clouds haul their stalled
evaporate overhead,

and below, on the lawn,
sprinklers rain
around themselves.
She's twelve, she's

just read *Anna Karenina*
and now the world's
a margin, the edge

of a better text.
                Below,
in the dusk, a woman
about to give birth

waits on the porch,
waits outside what
she feels, aware of
the body's comic aristocracy:

the shocked profile
above the belly, the belly
above the poor frightened feet.
She glances upstairs,

but upstairs there is
only Anna, who has given
her arm to the Commissar
of Darkness, her sleeve

brushing the sleeve
of the page with fire.
        The living page
crossed with blood

just one week before
by Raskolnikov—
                the print
ground like a servant's

studded heel in the face
of the status quo. So
what if this far south
of Siberia, the Aurora

diminishes to the cramped neon
                of a bar,
or here in the suburbs,
one star?

The neighbors' houses
loom dark as the inside
of a suitcase. The siren peels
its poisonous fruit, the seeds

scattering from the grave of Emma B.,
a black rain duplicating each pore
in her beautiful whorish face,
the absolute pronoun of that oval.

It will come to all of us,
the sky's empty parking lot
filled with glittering cinders,
the stillborn, the dead one,

standing next to each of us,
then aside. Like her eye
on the page, moving down the hall
on the arm of the blood machine,

the black dress walking on its own
to the hammered rails,
                    these words
waving two ways on the page,

like prayer,
            thank God
who with this book
in my hands
            keeps talking to me.

They are de-icing the Eastern shuttle.
Men in yellow masks stand on the wings
in the hard sleet and hose gold smoke
over the hold. The book on Cubism
in her hands shakes when they rev the jets.

She is going somewhere to teach somebody some-
thing, to talk to people sitting in solemn rows,
an orchard of note-takers, writing the words
dadaist disassociation over and over.

She can't find the page in her lecture notes
where Bergson says an image is the visual equivalent
of a musical chord . . . so maybe she can just walk
into the classroom, throw away the book and say:

Here's what your teacher did wrong in her life—
and here's what's wrong out there on the runway.

Look how we try to de-ice the surface,
in large-handed, smoky swipes at intimacy,
not getting down to the fragile metal,
the trouble-armor which, under nonstop,
high stress, disintegrates in thin air!

Something like these hands, students,
which have not held another body with love
in weeks. They hold the book to the heart,
defensively. They keep the fine, stylized
stream of interrogation flowing close to
the text, providing a pure reading of intention

similar to the recognition of hunger in another.
Or like a description of passion in language
utterly riveting, where what the author desires
beats so near to the surface.

If you love literature, question its critics—
who are to that beautiful effort as landing
gear and flaps are to the wings—

still extended beneath your teacher, holding up
as always, growing warmer now, by degrees.

The mind dislikes surprise.
Witness the nurse of good syntax,
how she pushes her drugged charges
across the courtyard below
to the Center for Impaired Speech.

Witness the doorman hesitating
before ringing your bell to tell you
someone's on the way up.

It's why you're getting up slowly
this morning, why you don't look too closely
at the mirror, nor the coffee table
offering its testimony: the matches

crippled in their books, crushed by
the insistent pressure of thumb and forefinger,
the empty fifth, the ZigZag litter,
the pages of unclothed women, legs apart,

smiling out as if there was no danger
in this world, even from those you love.
And from those who love you in ways you have
not yet imagined—and which might surprise you,

like a style of perverse instruction
say, teaching the blind pornography,
their trained fingers hesitating above
the machined welts of braille.

It is possible to teach someone that love
is pain—by taking a fistful of hair, pulling
it up from the skull and back, till the neck
locks in place, as if breaking, till the lover
stops thinking about politics, or the five days
of fine weather—and begins to cooperate
with this gesture, applied one night
in passion, the next in pure rage.

Still, the mind is stubborn, resists
the unexpected—shuttling back and forth,
as it was taught, between similar forms—refusing
in the only way it knows how, to make sense.

So you sit this morning, while the mail comes,
and the *Times,* the phone rings and you can touch
your hair, your face, rethinking it all—

       but recall your horror once
opening the front door, on your birthday, on seeing the faces
of your friends disfigured by the weight of occasion.
You thought the ones who liked you least screamed loudest:
Surprise!

AFTERWARDS

—L. (in memoriam)

After our short flight together,
we boarded separate planes
and flew to opposite ends of the country.

The first flight was rough,
you held me and later,
alone on the longer one, I recalled

the perfect gravity of your embrace,
and fell asleep, my dream blooming
backwards into the gentle silks of a chute.

Now, afterwards, I feel like I'm moving
obedient to some physical law people
believe in, but can never describe,
like the principle of air flowing over
the wings of a plane, allowing it to rise.

You sat beside me, holding me to
a perfect understatement of myself,
the way sign language understates thought
rediscovering it in the body.

Here, in another country, your thought
still holds me. You turn,
you say my name to me—
while the plane banks, as the tower dictates.

It has something to do with the power of loss,
how it opposes itself at the last moment.
It has to do with how the plane, lifting off

from this world reluctantly, reappears above it,
effortless in flight. It has to do with how

your lips felt smiling against my ear,
how you held me as we fell,
how falling together, our lives
seemed the only constant objects in the sky

and how impossible it seemed
that thin air would ever
begin to displace us.

A Fresco

All day I've been thinking of the grief
on each of their faces, Adam and Eve.

The feeling is closest to a wave as it peaks,
how it seems on the verge of self-consciousness

before it collapses. Their mouths hold
a single sound that divides, familiar as rain.

The angel points away from the green world
behind them, out into the nave. I remember

the woman standing there, turned to stone
at the side altar, and the man next to her,

the back of his overcoat on fire with
reflected light. They stared straight ahead

at The Expulsion and the cruel, distinct words
passed between them. Tourists, a corsage at her heart,

his brand new guidebook. What is startling
is how the fresco works itself out from under

the expectation of color. After a while
in this air, the other spectrum emerges:

no blues or reds but grades of dark and eerie
white, as the paint thins and the lead extracts

new expressions. They never raised their voices.
The woman seemed like someone who had been loved,

but without compassion. I don't know about the man.
I recall the rest of that church now, how

with small fierce gestures, votive fires
were lit. The two figures burning in effigy.

DAVID

He played a paralyzed man once,
before I knew him. He made
his body settle into
a position of broken readiness,

hunched on the rotting pins of his bones.
I thought I'd seen it before: actors
in wheelchairs as actors in wheelchairs.
But he gave that damage power,

a sound in the throat that rattled
the cast around him. Too real, I suppose,
for film, with its images fast as litter
in a ditch—but for me,

who'd been waking night after night
in a sweat of disbelief, my whole life
a Platonist double-take, sparkless
as the severed nerves of the spine,

it made sense. *Too real, I suppose,*
my moving hands on the bedclothes,
the good blood in my extremities,
some unwanted lover's love, gathered up

as he slept, into the repeating mechanism.
But that first morning, when we'd found
our way to each other, he'd already survived
my imagination and before dawn, I made

my pact with illusion. He was out
on the balcony and I thought
I heard singing. When I went out

there he stood looking over Assisi.
Not a single sound but the new sun,
a day, blue and windless,
coffee and a little bread on a tray.

WE DRIVE THROUGH TYNDALL'S THEORY OF SIGHT

—*David*

That day we drove for hours—
the blue clouds sculpted against the point
hundreds of miles away where architecture
seemed a promise. Still, as far as I can see,
we live in landscapes half-remembered:

the milky haze, the upturned eyes
of other lovers, light refracting
the impurities that make us
visible to each other.* The air itself
a form of resistance, a white grid

of retrospect—where a snowfall
of shadows shifts, forms people
we once knew, so perfect in their flaws.
Here is the world's skeleton: the ossified
white we have to imagine inside the body

clouded by such green eyes, such red lips,
a T-shirt that says DREAM ON. They could
make a movie of it: people who were mistakes,
people who held sentiment in fear, hostages
of their own commonness. Here, the horizon

seems to reenter itself and sing,
the way it once seemed to Sappho
at dusk addressing the Pleiades.

* Tyndall's Effect: that impurities in the air allow us to see light.

She looked at that rising city
and saw two things: stars made of dust

and those divine sisters made of the same.
This is how the poet saw and I say
you're perfect because I love you,
and also the reverse—though I catch you
beside me, shifting into fifth, with a beauty

Poe called supernal, feelings attached.
Make something of it, I dare you who read this.
We go forward into pure light, which
I am familiar with, though I also know
the Fat Man and the fox-faced woman,

I'm familiar with it all. This is as close
as we get on this earth, going forward,
transformed, into distance remembered.

The pure amnesia of her face,
newborn. I looked so far
into her that, for a while,

the visual held no memory.
Little by little, I returned
to myself, waking to nurse

those first nights in that
familiar room where all
the objects had been altered

imperceptibly: the gardenia
blooming in the dark
in the scarred water glass,

near the phone my handwriting
illegible, the patterned lamp-
shade angled downward and away

from the long mirror where
I stood and looked at
the woman holding her child.

Her face kept dissolving
into expressions resembling
my own, but the child's was pure

figurative, resembling no one.
We floated together in the space
a lullaby makes, head to head,

half-sleeping. *Save it,*
my mother would say, meaning
just the opposite. She didn't

want to hear my evidence
against her terrible optimism
for me. And though, despite her,

I can redeem, in a pawnshop
sense, almost any bad moment
from my childhood, I see now

what she must have intended
for me. I felt it for *her,*
watching her as she slept,

watching her suck as she
dreamed of sucking, lightheaded
with thirst as my blood flowed

suddenly into tissue that
changed it to milk. No matter
that we were alone, there's a

texture that moves between me
and whatever might have injured
us then. Like the curtain's sheer

opacity, it remains drawn
over what view we have of dawn
here in this onetime desert,

now green and replenished,
its perfect climate
unthreatened in memory—

though outside, as usual,
the wind blew, the bough bent,
under the eaves, the hummingbird

touched once the bloodcolored hourglass,
the feeder, then was gone.

SOUNDING

—for Annie Cameron

Four months in the womb
you were photographed
with sound. We stared

at the pulsing surface
of your skull, your fingers
lifting, as if to stave off

a sudden wind in that
sealed room where for
so long only our two

hearts echoed each other.
Screened, your heart glowed
at the joint of the caliper.

Months later, after
they had bathed you
and brought you to me,

I washed you again—
in privacy, opened
one by one the clenched

fingers seen too soon,
brushed the thin skin
of the skull where

the brain's leaping blood
bulged against it.
For months, I'd heard it

110

in dreams: the underwater gong
then the regular shock waves—
an assault as barbaric as conception,

the soul rung forward into image,
as metal is stunned into coin,
as the hammer sounds against its resistance:

the gold unblinking eye of the forge.

FROM *APPLAUSE* (1989)

DREAM

It's my old apartment, Gramercy Park,
but then it's not. I know the three steps up,
the squeaking door, the foyer table
stacked with mail, I know the light falling
like jail bars on the tiles, my numbered door.
But when I turn the key, there's a disco,
strobes, my dead landlord serving drinks.
Or it's a skating rink, a nook at the Frick.
Today I woke from sorting something in my head—
a box of old mittens or scarves,
snowflake patterns, shooting stars.
Here I have a poster on my wall:
the sun in shades, a turtleneck of smog.
It isn't just a dropped stitch,
my memory's actively unfurnishing that flat—
why I haven't a clue. But one, perhaps.
The time I stood, locked out,
on the snowy fire escape, looking through
the glass at my life: lamps, books,
coffee table, each self-contained photograph.
New York at dawn, even my flame silk dress
feels improvised now—it was that interior
I'd fix in my sight forever,
climb down the icy rungs and not come back.
Freezing wind out there, stocking feet,
my dress filling like a bell—
then a newer, dizzying grip on things,
this sudden hungry wish for riddance,
to turn my back on space I'd made,
with the pathetic charm of the possessive,
mine and uninhabitable.

AFTER CARE

You see the building falling down over there?
I come in to do my work when it's almost bare,

and if I may, I'll talk as I work,
washing the bodies of the dead squatters there,

under that sky the color
of a cigarette burn on a child's body.

In my line, I don't find
that too sensational a simile.
After care, after compassion

are outlasted by traffic
all night past the lit dock

of the morgue, after nobody
feels sorry for anybody anymore

it's there on the clockless wall
of the bar, the camera likewise
reducing death to the anecdotal:

the heap of small skulls down an airshaft
the infant dead at the starved mother's breast
forty days of blood spit in the torturer's dish
and what lies next to it . . .

what the righteous call the politics
of the matter, bent as they seem
on indenturing the dead to their rhetoric.

Unlike them, I am most useful
afterwards
taking a shroud measurement
sponging the blood
pressing out the small fires
along the scalp

and I tell you when I shut
those fierce eyes and draw
the expression somewhere between
surprise and sexual gratitude

I feel I've done what no one else
has with love—I've made the dead
for once, return it—

salvaged that last question
like a lock of hair thrown over
the shoulder, as each descends

the disappearing stairs.
I hold them up: eyes, lips, sexual wounds,
in what light we can still eke out of heaven
that bare swinging bulb under which

my hands work
for an effect we remember
long past compassion.

Where her right index fingernail should be—
there is a razorblade—
and the black-haired inmate pushes
the smaller one to the wall.

I remember it happening as I came
down the hall, with my copy
of *The Voice That Is Great Within Us*:

the two figures, one hunched over
the other, the blade hand hovering,
ablaze, then moving across and down.

Today, in the window,
a crystal spins on a bit
of fishline, throwing off light

like netted koi, shiny ruptures
on the ceiling. My small daughter climbs up
its trembling ladder,

extends her small beautiful hand.
In the perfect center of the glass
there is resistance to the image: a room

too brightly lit, in the basement
of the old House of Detention,
where I taught the dazzling inconsistencies—

Pictures in the Mind—
under the Watch Commander's
electric map: its red neon eye-slits

blinking each time a door cracked
within the walls. The women
gravely scrawling on Rainbow

tablets: not graffiti, but poems wrenched
from the same desire to own something—
to tie the tourniquet of style,

the mind's three or four known
happy endings clamped tight
on the jugular. Love poems to a pimp,

for example: she would never say
he beat her. No, he held her close,
he was "capable of love"—

he was like the elegy
written for the little one
whose mother tried to make her fly:

he would stay suspended in the air.
No one would see that child
screaming, step by step, along the gritty ledge.

If she'd lived, she might have become
the one who thought she wrote songs
like Billie Holiday, or the one

who plagiarized peacefully, week after week,
the poems of Langston Hughes.
Nobody writes anything that moves

across and down the face
of mortal anguish. That cutting tool
found in no book nor

in the exquisite, denatured vision
of invention—page after page
of Pictures in the Mind—but

I taught it right after all.
There were images for her,
                            this mother,

taking back the face she made—
with her bright revisionist blade—
too ugly, too fat, too stupid
to be loved

and an image for that sudden spidery blood
on the tiles, somewhere the red eye
tracking my impulse
as I pushed open the warning door,

then stood back, catching
the baby at the window—
her open hands, the moving light

she holds at the source
but cannot still.

When she came to visit me, I turned my face to the wall—
though only that morning, I'd bent my head at the bell
and with the host on my tongue, mumbled thanks.

Cranked up, then down in my bed—
I told the nurses jokes,
newly precocious, but too old

at twelve to be anything
but a patient. I slouched in my robe
among the other child-guests of St. Joseph,

the parrot-eyed scald masks,
the waterheads and harelips,
the fat girl with the plastic shunt.

The old crippled nun on her wheeled
platform dispensed her half-witted blessings,
then was gone like the occasional covered gurneys

sliding by my numbered door. *Gone*
told me I'd go away too—
orderly as dusk in the brick courtyard:

the blank windows curtained one by one.
I could not abide that yearning face
calling me home. Like the Gauls,

in my penciled translations: I saw
Caesar was my home. Through the streets
of the occupied city, his gold mask rose, implacable.

In the fervent improvisational style of the collaborator—
I imagined pain not as pain
but the flickering light embedded

in the headboard, the end
of the snake-wire uncoiling from
the nurses' station. The painkiller winked

in its paper cup, its bleak chirp
meant respect should be paid
for the way I too wielded oblivion,

staring at the wall till six,
gifts unopened in her lap,

the early dark deepening between us.

SKID

Where the snow effigies stood
hard-packed and hosed to ice
in front of the frat houses,
in the middle of the little bridge
over the stopped river,
my leased car spun three times

before the chainless tires caught.
Each time round I saw a face:
the man who imagined he loved me;
the woman who confided in me,
the child who cried "no" upon meeting me,
as if he saw at once to what use

we put those vanishing invented selves.
The slurred tracks, ringed dark
on the outbound path, froze and unfroze
for weeks after the party to celebrate spring.
Down the road, the local museum
considered the Ice Age. The glacier

slid in and out of its lit shape
through a fan of color transparencies,
each ray labelled with an age, a thaw,
the gauged bed of the moraine. Showed how
the ice junkheap hauled the broken shapes
in which we live, cave and gully and flat.

And a further dissolution, part of
a shape we would not recognize for centuries,—
like the coins that tumble down the dark slide

to the weighted spar that triggers the mechanism
that lifts the needle to the jukebox disk: "Blue Moon"—
you saw it standing like an atomic field,

charged with particles: little "you's" and "me's,"
estranged suddenly from the vanity of their motion—
and the prefigured feel of it, music and moon,
turning full force into its mindless will
then stopping, my foot on the accelerator.

Though my little daughter owns an Ideal farmyard
let me not direct her attention to
the bloody auction block, the rented backhoe
reversing the plow on the earth,
the iron of the farmer's hand dropped on nothingness.

I know that pain has its tradition,
the slaughtering blade,
the black blood pounded into the grain.
The dreaming animals that come to drink

at this trough understand no tradition,
but I can make the cattle speak
as mildly as they have ever spoken,
the night moths appear as harmless messengers.

The woman who is standing over there
under the tree near the fenceposts,
touching the carved initials—

she is harder to invent.
In a fairy tale, she would be the familiar,
privileged trespasser: she might even be what she is,
a former owner on disputed land.

See her eyes repossess the well,
the porch, the propped-up Ford?
A man in love with speed used to drive it,

its tailpipe a red comet
down the lonely roads. My daughter
wants to know who she is, how does she fit
in the picture, the green painted pasture?

Everyone thinks they can make her put down
the rags and the can of kerosene,
maybe the dear little local paper

will crown her queen of the burning trees,
the dynamited dam. It's written in
her two-word tattoo what she will do
and it's written to you

on such a bright night, moon on the fencepost,
the cow lowing softly, the ideal sky
split open suddenly with stars.

Issa's little daughter, Sato-jo,
on all fours in this haiku, laughs!
She's nearly my daughter's age
when he makes her immortal.

Her face contains his,
like a reflection of sun
that leaps from wave to wave—
still, if real age is in the expression,

she's sure enough of love
to have begun moving away.
One step, two. How the body
sways away from its origins,

the parents, the mourners,
who laugh and clap.
I look up into sunlight, Annie
in her flowered suit pressing

her hands on the moon rocket
printed on the bottom of the pool.
Two haiku, two seasons blown gently
apart by her breath: Sato-jo

dying of smallpox, Issa bending
over her, light surrounding them
like a moat. The burning wire
between them, silence: the same

soundless echo Hokusai paints
between the great wave, poised
and the fishing boats below.
And these, haiku: two opposed

notions of perfection:
the fat baby serene, New Year's Day.
Then autumn winds scattering
the red blossoms she loved to pluck.

Either her death or her life.
Neither will he liken to anything.
Not her soul to a kite.
Not the kite to a marker,

bearing the name of a child
running on the earth below it.
Nothing but water pouring into water.
Spring ending. How he holds her

in that moment before immunity,
before the dream
rises in its tree
of new bloomed resistance
into this future

where I wrap her in a towel,
I carry her in my arms.
I take her death into me
little by little—temple bells, grass—

happiness
when she smiles like this
when I see she'll live forever.

By day, she's not so sick. She hits
the hound, then kisses him: nice dog.
He cringes, then his wolfish face lights up.
To me, she does the same. At two, her love
of power's in two parts: love and power.
Late at night, I hold her to my breast—
the wet indent her fevered head makes
stays pressed against my gown. She doesn't
have to ask, I wake with her. I hold
the mercury up to the light and read
its red suspense, the little trapped horizon
of her heat. Her slowed lungs draw
and empty. Below, on the lawn,
a hunched figure—dawn?—rakes the black
grass light, turns into a set of swings,
I hold her sleeping weight and rock
till something in the east throbs up.
Day, offering itself, then drawing back.
Day, commuting from a city remote as hell,
or health, where I remember living once,
for myself. Long before this little bird
filled its throat outside the beveled glass,
before the headlines stumbled on the step.

—for Lynne McMahon

     In her bedroom,
she set a convex mirror on a stand,
so that when the visitor

     looked in
expecting to see the familiar
line of lip and brow,

     what appeared instead
was the head up-ended—
the mouth a talking wound

     above
the eyes, upside down, fluttering,
like the eyes in the skull

of a calf slung on the blood-hook—
or a baby's lightning blink, dropped low
in the bone cage about to be born

Walls washed down with the cold pardons of the nurse.
Gem green paint restored from old scrapings.
Here and there, a trifling, a lightening
beyond the author's original intent,
which was in the drawing room, positively spleenish.
From razor bits of palette, touch-ups: Mrs. Woolf's favorite
                                    color.

The Trust ladies place the still-ticking brain
of Leonard's wireless next to the empty brass stalk
with its single blossom: old black hat

she wore like pharaoh gazing down
the Nile-green Nile.
        That's her:
the flat drainboard of a face
set so fiercely against the previous
owner's trompe l'oeil beard and jug.

The simpleton's request: a picture of her *young*—
So the trees walk up burning,
the birds speak Latin
for the dull-witted, drenched palette

the glimpse of whirlwind in the pond
where their handfuls of ash
drifted down

            and over
the great mown meadow next door
where the Rodmell August Fair is on.
My daughter astride a steam engine,
bored as any child
with the past. Later makes an X
(her favorite letter) with two sticks

held up to the window
of the great writer's garden study.
But the mirror standing in the air
a glass knot tying and retying itself

would repolarize, and she, drawing near,
reverse herself. A woman's rapt beautiful face
drawn downward by gravity, sorrow,

lit upward by the flame of age—
could turn over, floating, then submerge, amniotic!

Across the green from the bedroom window
she saw it: a fin cleaving dark waters—
"and that became *The Waves*." The ladies sip and look.
        Vanessa, pregnant,
laughing, crosses the garden. Two women
walk among the hollyhocks with shears.
The hedge dented by one's fluttering hands.
Inside her sister's body: fluttering hands.

        Annie's white sweater catches
on the thorns of blackberry canes. I pull her free
then pick six little ones, busy, like the swarm cells
of a fetus. Or the enlarging failure in those rooms,
unchecked growth: death-drawn, claustrophobic.

The wind, up from the South Downs,
blew the two women across the garden,
their shadows like crossed sticks. Sisters.
One shrugging slightly, a loose mauve shawl.
Where her sculpted head sits now, a stone wall.

She sat at this table
eating mutton and bread.
He was talking about the socialist initiative
and she turned away: someone was knocking
at the window. It was the French photographer
we surprised on our way out,
shooting the forbidden
interior through the dark glass.

The man in the black suit delivers a eulogy
each page he turns, turns
a page of light on the ceiling,

because death mimics us, mocking
the eye's cowardly flight
from the flower-covered coffin

to the framed photo of the bereaved, alive.
It is not night.
It is California.

There are hibiscus dropping
their veined shrouds
on the crushed-stone path outside.

A gold cufflink blazes
as the eulogist raises his hands.

Shadows alter the ceiling,
the readable text.
There are two ways to meet death,

he says. *One fearful,
the other courageous.*
One day purposeful, the next hopeless,

A young man died because he had sex.
The eulogist speaks of soldiers under fire,
the cowards and the heroes.

The woman next to me cannot stop
weeping. I can find no tears inside
me. The cufflinks beam

signals at us, above us.
The sun through the skylight
grows brighter and brighter:

Watch now, God.
Watch the eulogist raise his hands.
The rays, like your lasers,

blind the front rows.
The gifts love gives us!
Some of us flinch, some do not.

EX-EMBASSY

*Sometimes, at dawn, I think I hear
the high sobbing cry of the muezzin
hanging in the sky before it's light
but then, I drop off to sleep again.*

Behind us is the ex-embassy.
Its pool a blue mosaic through
our hedge. The old man
in robe and wrapped head no longer

comes to mop the tiled edge—
his whole morning's work
fragmented by our wall of leaves.
No arm in a rolled sleeve,

bending, lifting. No flashing sections
of aluminum pole fit into a blue mesh scoop
for whisking up floating petals.
No closeup: like a Cubist inset,

a turbanned man sipping tea,
eyebrow and striped cup,
slice of a woman's profile
black half-veil, two eyes

yoked in kohl moving in a hand-held
mirror. No sun machine-gunning
that round of glass. No part
of a lamb turning on part of a spit.

No peacock opening a bit
of its promiscuous fan.
No cook hurrying the meat

with jagged curses. No meat.
No god. No medallion front,
officially defaced,
        the cornices deflagged
as bare crude evidence
or our power to invade,
theirs to resist.

A For Sale sign likens it
to a house on a cloud,
a sunrise mosque. It has
patterned tiles with sickles

of wheat or hashish. And wickets,
a *porte cochère* engemmed
with rotating spots.
Maybe a neighbor, through

a closing door,
saw grown men cry out
in a frenzy, on a cold floor,
to a god no one comprehends.

No one comprehends how,
like the god of the broken, rusted lamp,
once out, uncramped,
                    he's *not*.

Not anything you could imagine
not any servant

but the familiar reductive infinite—
lines of fuel drums, phone wires.
Rolled up in the bottom of a child's red valise,

timing devices, threads of plastique . . .
left behind for the doubters,
the personal grit of some other deity,
some intoxicating tattooed Allah

above the human ruins, head in hand.
Not that. Not this. In the garden,
a broken rope of amber beads,
within each separate bead
the lights of patrols go by,
elongate—the next night and the next—

            what I don't know
            but learn to dread
            turns over slowly in my bed.

—for Paul Monette

1

Not the glittering shudder in the ear, the high whine of
                                        the wasp,
Not the drunk holding up a glass, getting eloquent; nor
percussive, furious, the steady drum on the desk of the child

who doesn't get it. Not the echoing blow to the right temple
of the guard patrolling the green lawns of the industrial giant,
the hail of stones and beer cans onstage at the rock concert—

nor the thunk-thunk of a pistol whipping,
the eerie scree of someone screwing gun to silencer.
Applause has no opposite, contains its own poles—
yet it might be said the soundlessness of the newly dead,

the preternaturally silent chorus of, in this news photograph,
a family, (drowned on their way here from Haiti) is audible.
still afloat, lashed to their tiny illegal raft—hands folded
together, like this, like applause for the end, the soul's
                        tortured bow and exit.

2

Applause has a place: punctual comment,
forever hearing itself, even in a mob. As if clapping
is thought, a glass hatch high above everything, but
occasionally caught off-guard— like the woman or man
who moves air traffic across the skies, psyching out
the 3-D screen, piping the buzz in the earphones direct
to the pilots. Those steady voice blips, split suddenly with deific
      chitter,

surprise! God is a space chimp, communicating
from his little phobic cell circling earth, razzing the planets.
Intercepting the perfunctory handoff, airport to port,
the altitude drift—God the screecher, god the stomper,
God the whistler in the balcony: they listen to plain static,
hungry for his holy voice, his Bronx cheers. God in his tiny
monkey spacesuit, chewing up the tubes of all the technology
he never mastered, God the Glitch, clapping his ugly furry little
      mitts.

3

You're clapping. In the photo for Holly's* exhibit,
one shot of each subject, face and hands, maybe thirty in all,
each photo on the wall of a circular room and the people
photographed are applauding. If you stand in the center
of that room, they applaud *you*.

                        Nice conceit. Nice comment
on perspective. Nice immediate drift toward the philosophical.
Like Goya, the pure strain on the image can bend to political
                                     argument.

See that fat man clapping? He's mean, he doesn't want to do it,
but others are, so he tries to make his rhythm revisionist, one
                            half second off.
See the other guy, preoccupied, going over his bills in his head
as he claps? Or the woman in the flowered hat, thrilled
to be an audience, thrilled to be a pair of long, black theater
                      gloves, one thrilled glass eye?

* Holly Wright, photographic exhibit, "Applause"

4

Straight into the eyes of you, a real close-up,
making those palms applauding an unnatural act—
but so what? you seem to say. Your gaze labors to be direct:
too aware of the ironies of the so-called candid shot.
You look like a theatergoer, lit by the shifting prism
of stagelight. Ladies, gentlemen, the audience takes
its seat in familiar anonymity, but wait—
your hands keep meeting in midair.
You don't stop clapping, even after the others do.
That's who she photographed, seventh row, no heckler,
but you in that instant you don't stop, you go on
applauding every moment, though I know that's my projection.
Because your friend is in the photograph next to you—
still alive then, so joyous, I don't think I've ever seen a man
                                    look that happy.

5

I suppose it happened something like this.
A woman got up (because the moon was full, because
her newborn was going to live now, after all, because
the fire of dung and grass did not, for once, go out)—
and began to dance. She moved her hips inside the animal skin,
the firelight made her look so huge that he loved her
and wanted just to see her there attached to her great shadow.
Seeing her shuffle and hop, he started to make a sound
with his hands. She looked up. It was not the slap of bare feet
on stone, not the bones of the dead in the wind, but a bearded
ugly appreciator she would come to call by name. He was saying
with his hands: I am looking at you and you are my delight
and this sound makes clear who I am. I am the one watching
you and saying it is good, making my two hands the collision of
love and power.

6

Grape laboring over grape out of dark green leafage,
out of the woven balsa strips of the scuppernong, set
against the white stucco wall of the garage, set off-kilter
like a leaf crown sliding over the eye of Bacchus. Years later,
in Perugia, in the blue valley at wine harvest, I found
the sweet life-source of it, that image, the bare-bottomed
children in the mother's arms, the vat of grape, the handclap
at dusk in the cobbled street: *come home.* The day of his
funeral, I noticed the arbor near the Chapel of Memory,
rife with pale blue-green grapes against the white tiles. I
didn't think of wine, or new-minted money—I thought of
a shift downward from thought as they brought the coffin past,
a cliché of hearing: waves, cicadas, or the wind's slow applause
through the graveyard trees—it was just that sound seemed so
necessary—a dog barking, a plane—something of this life to
                                        salute him, anything.

7

Well, what did we expect? You and I
were joking once that the self is a path
of stepping-stones sinking in the black water:
now the self is nothing more than a sound.
Like the dawn rain, *om,* anahat, 4th chakra,
the sound of two things *not* hitting
together. Annie draws faces in the air with her finger,
expects us to see who and where they are, say
excuse me when I walk through them. *Excuse me,*
I'm walking through my mother and father, Jesus,
Coco Chanel, Torquemada, Saint Athanasius,
and Simone Weil, poets living and dead, *excuse me*—
sound waves of one person standing up,
clapping the whole time, not for an encore, but for
                                    the end of it.

8

In irresistible eclipse, two shadow jets converge
on the cypher-green screen: the controller spills
his coffee, screaming into the mouthpiece of the headset.
Gets drifting static, the wind, night, fog. He
doesn't see the sky light up once, twice, two hundred
miles south, but he sways in place and calls them to him:
pilot, flight attendants, the woman in the fifteenth row
nursing her infant, the toddler racing up and down the aisles
(stopped forever midstride), the elderly vacationers,
the whole living matrix, sitting tight in a horseshoe,
flung out there beyond direction. Huddled like an audience,
or the gallery of people pictured applauding, while
the dark figure in the spotlight beckons—they stay so animated,
refusing to imagine it: the act of relinquishing thought,
then joining whatever it is in that huge specific light onstage.

9

Walked in to polite applause. (The teacher-keepers
had insisted: *be nice or else.*) Thirty-six or so
teenage mothers, runaways, JD's, misfits, abused
babies. They looked, at first, like one big leer:
Impress us, poet-ess. (God, should I read Plath?)
Then it came back to me: the raw gleam of those nights
at Rikers. Poems of the oil spill, the ruptured tanker
roiling on the top-water, sullen ink of the inmates' fingers.
Then a torch hits the slick: flames
skyscraper-high. These brows furrow the same,
they write their Letters to God, Mamma, or an Unborn
Child. Here's a hurt girl, head down, reading hers—
from a dead kid. "Don't do what my mama did
to me, with drugs:—*I was like a butterfly wrapped
in a cocoon. She cut my wings, then my eyes, she ripped
my five senses, she wove that white powder into my shroud.*"

10

It was After Care, the name of the program,
some obscure branch of New York City services.
Our job: to find jobs for "ex-offenders," newly ex.
A simple task? For a twenty-four-year-old
student of Marcuse, enemy of the state? Piece of cake.
Fast talk. I called up Chase Manhattan—
You mean you *don't* want to hire a first-class
booster to work in the vault? Or Ma Bell:
Good with numbers I said of the hooker in front
of me. Ma said no, so did the hooker. Why should
she scrape for ninety bucks a week when a good night
brought six hundred? *Dumb flatback!* She sneered,
when a friend said she wanted to go straight.
"You sittin' on your money-maker!" I heard that quote over
and over that hot summer, on the phone, sweating.
I sat flat on my money-maker, using my big money-loser
to rethink economic politics. But then, I've always been
surprised to find the world just the way the cynics made it.

11

What happens to that youthful formality of purpose?
(I feel like I'm lost, do you? Listening to everyone
applauding a play I missed.) Spring here in L.A. today,
ninety or so, everything in bloom. I drive my four-
year-old to preschool and turn off Santa Monica
into a stakeout. Top-lit cop cars jackknifed onto lawns,
a chopper churning the smog, an amplified voice:
Come out with your hands raised. Listen up.
My kid doesn't look up from her book, *The Big Orange Splot.*
Police phrasing doesn't phase her.
I stare at a woman on the curb, solemnly applauding
—as if this is a film set. Perhaps it is.
But who was in that house? I woke, wondering
today. Who's in my life in this cracked white temple, L.A.?

12

Each day's lack of point is why we lower ourselves
between armrests in the false dark to see what some
overpaid auteur lusts after. We go on because of the
lack of distance applause lends to distance—we clap
not so much to judge as to be that other character,
the one offstage who knows the most—therefore most hurt,
pleased, or estranged. Applauding applause. One day a while
before he died, you came over with him. Annie was napping
in her crib and he touched her head and said
sleep well honey. I wanted to cheer him for going on
like that, for blessing my child when he knew he was dying—
and when the raft hit the swells, one after the other;
they held on and prayed and God laughed, God gave them
   a hand.
That was what God liked most, circling in his capsule,
when they beamed the messages out of the great radio
                          telescopes—
We're here, here's a picture of us, third from the sun,
here's DNA, a human baby—and a V for peace!
He sent them his holy static, from all the way back
to the Bang, when he first thought of it, the sound of clapping,
on the seventh day, as he sat back, as he rested.

FROM
RED TROUSSEAU
(1993)

TO THE MUSE

New Year's Eve, 1990

She danced topless, the light-eyed drunken girl
who got up on the bow of our pleasure boat
last summer in the pretty French Mediterranean.

Above us rose the great gray starboard flank
of an aircraft carrier. Sailors clustered
on the deck above, cheering, and the caps rained down,

a storm of insignia: U.S.S. *Eisenhower*.
I keep seeing the girl when I tell you
the *Eisenhower*'s now in the Gulf, as if

the two are linked: the bare-breasted dancer
and a war about to be fought. Caps fell
on the bow and she plucked one up, set it rakishly

on her red hair. In the introspective manner
of the very drunk, she tipped her face dreamily up,
wet her lips, an odalisque, her arms crossed

atop the cap. Someone, a family member, threw a shirt
over her and she shrugged it off, laughing, palms
fluttering about her nipples. I tell you I barely knew

those people, but you, you liked the girl, you
liked the ship. You like to fuck, you told me.
The sex of politics is its intimate divisive plural,

we, us, ours. *Who's over there?* you ask—*not us.*
Your pal is there, a flier stationed on a carrier.
He drops the jet shrieking on the deck. Pitch dark:

he lowers the nose toward a floating strip of
lit ditto marks and descends. Like writing haiku—
the narrator is a landscape. A way of staying subjective

but humbling the perceiver: a pilot's view.
When you write to your friend I guess that
there are no margins, you want him to see

everything you see and so transparent is
your kind bravado: he sees that too. Maybe
he second-guesses your own desire to soar over

the sand ruins, sit yourself in the masked pit
and rise fifteen hundred screaming feet a minute
into an inaccessible shape: falcon, hawk—Issa's

blown petals? Reinvent war, then the woman's faithless
enslaved dance. Reinvent sailors bawling at the rail
and the hail of clichés: flash of legs on the slave deck.

Break the spell, reverse it: caps on the waves as they
toss away their uniforms, medals, stars. Then the girl
will wake up, face west, a lengthening powerful figurehead

swept gold with fire. The waves keep coming: the you, the me,
the wars. Here is the worst of it, stripped, humiliated—
or dancing on the high deck, bully-faced, insatiable.

Here is the lie that loves us as history personified,
here's the personification: muse, odalisque, soldier,
nightfall—swear to us, this time, you will make it right.

LUCIFER

Two A.M. and we're on Lucifer, arguing, drinking,
one of us a Believer. I say if that beautiful
light-named angel, once most loved of God,
fell, he must have kept falling into insight—
scattering his illumination, plummeting, coming apart
into a broken new deity, one that divides
as the woman's face in darkness,
the man's face in quick rip-slashes of light.
Starry dark: down and down She falls into her empty glass,
the night sky lights up with all He refuses to let go.

These beads are hot, my daughter says,
lifting them gingerly from my neck—somehow
ignoring the obvious: they're pretty and they're red.

These are the days of pre-school entrance tests. Some
nitwit reads a *text,* asks kids to give it back verbatim.
The beads are hot, my daughter says,

touching the ring of red glass planets
warm from pooling at the throat's steady pulse.
Ignoring the obvious: that they're pretty and they're red—

she says instead what's usually left unsaid.
In her model galaxy, Earth pushes back Mars.
The beads (strung on hanger wire) are hot, she says:

aligned in sequence from the bulb's too-
steady glare. *Hot* she says, moving Earth, moving Mars,
ignoring the obvious: one's pretty, one's red.

We can't say why our minds orbit this Earth, can we, kids?
Or why Mars looks mean as Hell! Blood leaps in the neck.
These beads are hot, my daughter says.
Ignoring the obvious: they're pretty. And they're red.

Stuck pat with strawberry magnets
to her sub-zero are all the stages:
gill slits, lungs, sex—stopped
at the third month, when the fetus

is sucked out into a clear plastic bag.
Reaching in for a quick soda, you can almost
feel that flexible wind on your face.
The fetus (named *Jennifer*, it says)

develops in color-photo sequence till the second
trimester, when (more bold-face) the kid's
a murder victim, in cold blood, of Mom. You beckon
to nothing: milk cartons, cans, stand in the chill blast

of the suction door and grab your Sprite.
Day and night she stands outside the clinics
with the other Lifers. My advice: don't
take her on. I once learned phylogeny

provides intelligent options—but survival
does not always select for insight.
Down the line: there's a smug printed
sign talking up adoption. Right.

So, knocked up, I'd owe my body to
an unforgiving god, who'd swallow my offspring
too? Here's a fat man rattling a blood red
genie in a pickle jar. No wedding ring.

See that woman, head bent—they're hurrying her
through the police cordon, past the screaming faces?
I've walked where she's walking now—
and where she lies now, I once lay,

behind that secured door, near that white
waiting table. My mind divided, momentarily,
as if the world were just birth or no birth,
what I could or could not do and still seem

human to myself. Who first fixed in
my head that slashed membrane between life
and death? (I'd go toe-to-toe against her,
but she stops me cold with her small, past due

figure of remorse.) *God, what next?* she asks,
leaning against her icebox, her T-shirt
shouting how she pities the unborn. So do I.
But not as much as I pity her, quickening

with hate. And *love:* for those would-be
lives inbred to a set of family
gestures. One day on our way to the frog
pond we take my daughter's hands, saying

nothing—one on each side. She
asks me why I don't see what she believes.
I want to say *I do,* I see through all the cross-
wielding apologists to why she, alone in her kitchen, grieves.

It's sad. The big frogs croak like TV preachers
pad to pad. But look: at the pond rim
she points out tadpoles—hundreds, ink-black, legless.
See? we both say. My daughter kneels, tries to cup them

in her fist, but they're too fast. Born again and
again into the limits of our perception, they swim
intuitively, the way we think. She calls that
revelation. We're surrounded by the bull

chorus, a booming, backlit percussion. *Call
it revelation* she says aloud, and I won't, though
I'd call it the soul of a woman. Not the one she
discovers at conception. No, *this one,* this

split-cell insight, sister, sister,
this raw fixed light in her face set to mine.

LITTLE L.A. VILLANELLE

I drove home that night in the rain.
The gutterless streets filled and overflowed.
After months of drought, the old refrain:

A cheap love song on the radio, off-key pain.
Through the maddening, humble gesture of the wipers,
I drove home that night in the rain.

Hollywood sign, billboard sex: a red stain
spreading over a woman's face, caught mid-scream.
After months of drought, the old refrain.

Marquees on Vine, lit up, name after name,
starring in what eager losses: he dreamed
I drove home that night in the rain.

Smoldering brush, high in the hills. Some inane
preliminary spark: then tiers of falling reflected light.
After months of drought, the old refrain.

I wanted another life, now it drives beside me
on the slick freeway, now it waves, faster, faster—
I drove home that night in the rain.
After months of drought, the old refrain.

FIELD TRIP

Downtown, on the precinct wall,
hang the maps of Gang Territories,
blocks belonging to the red Bloods
or blue Crips. Colored glass hatpins

prick out drive-by death sites—
as the twenty-five five-year-olds
pass by. They hold each other's hands
behind their tour guide, a distracted

man, a sergeant, speaking so far over
their heads, the words snap free
of syntactical gravity: *perpetrator,*
ballistic. The kids freeze in place,

made alert by pure lack of comprehension.
Then, like the dread Med fly, they specialize:
touching fingerprint pads and then their faces,
observing the coffee machine (the plastic cup

that falls and fills in place), the laser printer
burning in the outlines of the Most Wanted
beneath a poster of a skeleton shooting up.
It's not so much that they are literal minds

as minds literally figurative: they inquire
after the skeleton's health. To them a thing
well imagined is as real as what's out the window:
that famous city, city of fame, all trash and high

cheekbones, making itself up with the dreamy paints
of a First Stage Alert. The sergeant can't help
drawing a chalk tree on the blackboard. He wants
them to see that Justice is a metaphor, real as you

and me. Where each branch splits from the trunk,
he draws zeros and says they're fruit, fills each
with a word: arrest, identification, detention,
till sun blinds the slate. Not far away, through

double-thick glass, a young man slumps
on a steel bench mouthing things, a clerk
tallies up personal effects. Now he comes
to the gangs, how they own certain colors

of the prism, indigo, red—he doesn't tell
how they spray-paint neon FUCKS over
the commissioned murals. The kids listen
to the story of the unwitting woman

gunned down for wearing, into the war zone,
a sunset-colored dress. She was mistaken
for herself: someone in red.
She made herself famous, the way people

do here, but unconsciously—becoming
some terrible perfection of style,
(bordering as it does, on threat.)
The sergeant lifts his ceramic mug,

etched with twin, intertwining hearts,
smiling like a member of a tribe. Later,
on the schoolroom floor, the kids
stretch out, drawing houses with chimneys,

big-headed humans grinning and waving
in lurid, non-toxic crayon. Here is
a policeman, here a crook. Here's a picture
of where I live, my street, my red dress.

                    Our planet, moon. Our sun.

The drunk next to her on the plane
holds up the photograph for her to witness:
an eight-year-old in braids
stolen away from him by an unspeakable
ex, through paid-for testimony.

Under her tongue, a milled tablet turns,
ready to separate the body from its terror
of motion, strapped to a seat
before a spread tray. His Scotch sits
jiggling in a cup-shaped niche, impaled

by a reading ray. His mouth opens
above the red slash of his silk tie.
He imitates, hand flat, a plane
taking off—*zoom*—so split

the wife and child. Then to show how
they broke him, he slumps in his seat.
Together, they watch his made-up plane
bank before the dropping movie screen.

Now it's dark. His drink flashes in the blue-
and-flesh beams shot from the credits.
His hands work in the air before Pompeii:
a long shot of ancient courtyards and whole

families frozen in domestic poses. One fall,
he says, flashing a wound, a torn screen scarred
him. He was only putting on storms.
Before us, the time-traveler turns an Uzi

on the plane, the robot girl cracks a smile.
Turbulence: the meal tray shakes under
the hand of the raconteur: one, two, three:
steak and rhubarb mousse. The air chops

like his hand, but all faces stay stubbornly
turned from him—including her face, daring him.
Every motion a betrayal, every gesture a fall into fire.

What is woman but a foe to friendship . . .

—*Malleus Maleficaram*
(Witches' Hammer, 1494)

1

Because she desired him,
and feared desire, the room
readied itself for judgment:
though they were nothing to
each other, maybe friends,
maybe a man and a woman
seated at a table
        beneath a skylight
through which light poured,
interrogatory.

2

Because his face always appears to her
half in shadow,
                    she chooses finally
to distrust him and her seared memory,

even though it was noon, when the sun
hovers in its guise of impatient tribunal,
seizing every contradiction in dismissive brilliance:

the white cloth, their separate folded hands,
a mock-crucible holding fire-veined blossoms. No,
it was a bowl of fruit, a glass of red wine,
the simplest, thoughtless vessel, that was it,
wasn't it, held up, like this, an offering?

3

Reading the account of the trials,
late at night, she sees that the questions
must have begun in a friendly, almost desultory
fashion: rising slowly in pitch and intensity,
to reveal, finally, God's bright murderous gaze,
the mouth of the trap. Conviction required stigmata,
the search for the marks of Hell's love on the un-male
body, the repetitive testimony of men: that she midwifed
the stillborn, curdled milk, spied, screamed at climax,
grew wings—and worse, *Looking over her shoulder,*
I saw her laughing he said *laughing at me*

till, at the end, days later, she could feel
her way eagerly, blind, cleansed of memory,
through the maze of metal doors to the last door:
                    the single depthless mirror.

4

They were already disappearing, sitting there together
talking in a forthright way, laughing, unaware of their faces
reflected, enlarged like cult images, effigies:
dark hair, light hair. Already the ancient lens
sliding into place between them, whose purpose is not
to clarify sight, but rather to magnify, magnify till
                its capacity for difference ignites.

    Tell me why it was only his gaze on her,
why his right to primary regard, *her* life under scrutiny,
her life reduced to some fatal lack of irony, naive midwife
                    to this monstrous *please?*

      See how the lens bends the light
into what amounts now to tinder . . .

      So sight can come, now, heatedly alive,
               living wood, corrected.

5

I admit now that I never felt sympathy for her,
as she stood there burning in the abstract.
Though condemned by her own body
(the ridiculous tonsured hair, bare feet
and bruised cheek, as if she'd been pushed up
against a headboard in passionate love)—
I suspected her mind of collaboration,
apperceptive ecstasy, the flames wrapped
about her like a red trousseau, yes,
the dream of immolation.

But look at the way her lips move—
it is the final enlightenment. Below
the nailed sign of her craft
                    are the words published
from her lover's mouth
the mouth of the friend who betrayed her:
her naked body, his head on her breast
like a child's, *heal me,*
and her answer?

God, tell me there was a moment
when she could have willed herself in to language,
just once, into her own stammering, radical defense:

I am worth saving

before the flames breathed imperious at her feet
before her mouth, bewitched, would admit to anything.

1

My sister is painting not painting
slapping her brush across the air's smug expression,
            whipping pointillist grit
            ahead of her unseen broom

flung into the split hoof of the dustpan:
invisible pictures.
            Invisible man, invisible woman,
breath-colored bones, hair, cunt and cock.

            On the mirror she paints glass bricks,
each with a woman's face inside,
            mouth open, not screaming.

She flicks the brush, skin-painting
over her belly, over the unborn body within,
            future shapes of desire:
            arms, legs, sex, blinking heart.

She laughs: *Is this Minimalist enough?* I watch her,
drinking coffee. Somewhere, they're planning to pass
laws against mimicry—especially such extreme mimicry:
painting, not painting, birth, no birth at all.

2

This one is the most beautiful: a waterfall.
She painted herself here, standing just
behind the pour, a thin glassy sheet.
She was playing captive, winking:
red mouth, naked, necklace of dragonflies.

I remember that day and
this embarrassed meal,
the elongated utensils,
punctured orange sun.
She painted everyone's
anguished silence—
just after Uncle, drunk,
had disgraced himself
by telling his awful story.

     She painted a parrot,
neon-green, on Uncle's head.
Shamed by his small vocabulary,
he couldn't help himself.
Two of his phrases were
Prove it and *Fuck Freud.*

The parrot, not the uncle.

3

He'd trained it. Was the parrot obscene?
He said other things: shit, hell, piss.
A family scandal. When he sat on Uncle's shoulder,
he projected his metal voice into Uncle's
human one, telling his famous story, helplessly,
after a shot or two. All of us staring into our plates.

Aunt Grace, his wife, drank gin fizz
from a tall glass, peering at
the clear, bloodcolored swizzle
stick like a thermometer.

                    But there was no stopping him.
He was back in the War, last one left
in his regiment, wintry Alps, everyone dead around him.
He buried no one, but waited days and days to be saved.
He dreamed they were alive in a different way. He sang.
Suddenly he saw a young man in a military uniform, standing
before him in a bright light. Then the youth's clothes
melted away and the boy became a woman.
                              Uncle desired him,
desired to lie down with her among the dead bodies

of all his friends who had died for our country.
The man-woman turned away, then faced him again,
revealing the Sacred Heart burning in its cage
                              of neon thorns.

Carried at last down the mountain
to the hospital, he could not stop
seeing this, telling this.

               So Christ was a woman
and he longed to fuck her. God is the two
sexes joined, he cried, spilling,
don't you see, one sex! joined at the heart!

4

Till they held two wires to his temples
(obscenity, sacrilege) and he grew quiet,
walled up in the family business, a man
in a glass elevator—moving his jaws
enough to be male: some hellos, dirty jokes.
                    But a flurry of gestures:
hands pressed to his temples, dead thumbs on a buzzer,
fist raised, snatching at air as if he could
catch his story, lightning in the shifting,
cloudy synapses. He put out his hand for
a firm handshake, a backslap, then secretly raised
his middle finger, scratching his nose.

Years later, he looked up, seeing his niece
beside him, calmly sketching.
Not talking to him, just sketching,
the pencil tracing the shapes of the thorns
eating each other around that red and blue
                    beating suspension.

5

She lives in a little town. She's afraid.
She imagines herself facing some ignorant, powerful
tribunal:
       giving advice on how not to paint.
Terrific, she says, how *not* to paint this story:
Not paint *here:* the snow riddled with holes,
shrapnel pocks, little yellow lacework of piss
or *here,* not paint Uncle bearded, raving
on his knees? Not paint *here,* his friend, the corpse,

boots and helmet, mouth open in song—half of
a silent aria, the cement duet of *pain, sky, pain,
sky?* Here. Not paint the soldier-christ-woman
with her removable heart atorch, her black brassiere,
sheer black stockings?
              Not paint *here,* the center,
bruisecolored, tumescent, his bloody hand on himself?

6

Well then, *not* the sky's flaming torso, sunset,
or the shaking puzzles of fire I saw when you slammed
the screen door's gold mesh between us—
                                        years ago—
                                        that summer dusk?

Not the blessed anarchy of your teasing face,
screaming *I can paint things you've never dreamed of!* Or
me, screaming back, yanking the door, wild
with joy and insult, *You mean the blind can paint?*

Then who will paint us noticing how
he stood there, across the lawn,
a glass burning in one hand? In the other,
the creature in its gold cage, all swirling feathers . . .

and the beak, the terrible slit tongue, don't you
remember? backing us up to what we'd always be?
Prove it—then the other thing, remember it? Or not?

                    the joke, the obscenity?

PRAGUE: TWO JOURNALS (1970, 1990)

*—Jan Palach, a Czech student, burned himself to
death protesting the 1968 Soviet invasion of Prague*

AVENUE OF STATUES, CHARLES BRIDGE, 1970

Look at her, St. Somebody-or-other:
clutching her stone roses
like some ancient maid-of-honor.
A big girl who elbowed boldly up
to catch the bride's bouquet. She
caught the future: *it wasn't hers.*
        The statues tremble:

see it? a blue spasm, like a wave, breaking over
the rigid faces, the stone musculature. Eye-flicker
of intent, maybe the sculptor's last gesture
completing itself in the unsettled stone? What
            was just beyond the chisel's inference—

a long luxurious stretch, arms up, a yawn,
a bared breast. The shoe falls: what happened next.

History, like a bus, stopped and let us off
in a pool of some light substance, stones of air.

        A little crowd of long-hairs,
after curfew, out of our depth—it slowly dawns on us,
            we're somewhere important!

A trail of rose-lit tents on the horizon,
and these saints with their raised spears:
                    sunrise.

Havel's face everywhere, my daughter's hand in mine.
The street jammed all the way to the National.
I look for a plaque, a sign commemorating
his death. An old man, a bureaucrat, quietly pops corks,
carves ice wedges into swans, dolphins, girls—
hunched over an old file cabinet he's wrestled
to the curb. Snowy commas curl from his knife.
No plaque. No sad past tonight. A street singer
tries sleight-of-hand, but her cards are frayed.
Heretics ignite the images. Years make clear
their courage: they stood alone saying there's
a better god or forget god—refine an image,
worship it, refuse to go blind: see my numbered face?
All this faceted chance: diamonds, hearts.
My daughter watches the parade of cards, marked. I remember
how they covered the spot where he burned with rough pine.
It became, nevertheless, an off-limits shrine.
What's in the file under his name?
            A pile of ashes. A glass of cheap champagne.

CHARLES BRIDGE, 1970

Hey Jude some kids intone at the sound of boots.
Did we think we'd go limp, recite Marcuse? Embossed flash
of a Red star, then a bullhorn's raised note.
We left right away. A student visa gets me to Kafka's grave,
but we're forbidden to sit among these thirty hooded figures,
of catch Z's like that sleeper in the shadow of a raised
stone axe, pass around hash in a flat pipe.
The weary mind closes its eyes behind the stone masks.

   I woke up, dreaming an eye painted
over the missing breast of St. Ludmilla,
protector of the outsider, the circling soul.
I dreamed I saw Jan Palach's ghost.
Who'd nothing to say to us, though I watched him
for a sign as he crossed. Beneath his feet,

the bridge hovered like a spacecraft on its sixteen pillars,
built to last: pink-lit, spanning the Vltava.

FAUST HOUSE, 1970

In this house lived Edward Kelley, the English alchemist,
who transmuted gold at the court of Rudolf Two.
To a pound of boiling mercury, he'd add a single
drop of blood-red oil and beckon the court,
                    come see the brilliant grit in the pot!

Today soldiers reinforced the planks
over the spot. There was a girl there
who'd been his intimate. She'd cried but said nothing.
I saw his photograph, laughing. First the blood-red powder
added to the boiling contents of the crucible—
then you can just make it out
        through the colored smoke, bits of stars,
        spittle, a horse's bit, a blow to the sweet footman's skull:
                                            gold.

GOLDEN LANE, 1990

Alchemist's Lane. Mouse-houses, sixteenth century. Frowning
under the castle arches. Goldbeaters, so called, fled here from
a fire. Up this diminishing street comes me, twenty years ago,
clutching my Duino Elegies. Flutter of silk at my neck. I could
recite all the once-resident writers: Seifert, Maranek, Kafka—
neighbors of Madame de Thèbes the fortune teller and a man who
                              owned a circus of white mice.
Later, at the hotel, I call an old phone number and then another.
I put weight on one boot-heel, showing off my Bohemian
    ancestry,
college politics. Who would I be next? A voice says hello in
    Czech,
then speaks English. Palach put in his pocket: a political tract,
a poor flower. Then the flames re-made him. Hello. My name is
                              Carol.

THE CLEMENTINUM, 1970

At the Clementinum, I am shown the Latin hymnal on
  parchment—
dirty words in Czech scribbled in the margins
by the noble ladies of St. George Convent. I'd give
my left tit to read this: Prague's earliest record of smut
written in the vernacular. By ladies. In a holy book. Well,
they were sick of the Empire, sick of the foreign liturgy.
Sick of being skirts. A pox on the rump of the fat Roman
priest! Jan Hus, the clear-eyed heretic,
threw out the sacristy's Papist gold.
Ladies, I give you the Roman Church, he said in Czech,
                                        and struck the match.

He burned fast, she said to me today,
the girl who was Jan Palach's lover.

HOTEL INTERCONTINENTAL COFFEE SHOP, 1990

In the Intercontinental Coffee Shop my daughter
rips her red lollipop free of a linen napkin,
reminding me suddenly of a rude passage I once glued
in an etiquette book. Something about the private parts
of Emily Post, a little kid's revenge—
though I still hate etiquette lessons. A jacket-back goes by,

the Soviet symbol with a bar through it.
Get it? says Annie, popping
her gum. *Down with red stars.*

Across the table from us is Jan Palach's lover.
In hat and scarf, though it's warm—
her face still young, but worn, like a book paged through
by cynics. She talks fast, catching up to an old self.

CHURCH OF OUR LADY OF TYN, 1970

Here's the marker for Tycho Brahe,
the Danish astronomer who believed the earth
was the center of the universe. *Better to be*
than to seem to be was the motto carved in his headboard.
Outside, a light rain begins to fall. The girl at my side
tells me that her lover stuttered, *a slight impediment*
she says. But when he sang foreign rock: Blowin'
in the Wind, Satisfaction, there was no hesitation.
That day he died, he sang a song
he'd made up. It rhymed but when she tries
to think of it, it's gone, even in Czech
there are only commas. Tycho set the self
a task: an orbit defied. So in the mirror, he saw the face
floating to the left in its ring of flames, detached.

I kissed his arms, she says, the little hairs stood up.
Then we went out together, into the street.

As she talks, I see her crossing the chalk lines
drawn shakily on the stones of the Square. He lengthens
beside her: the shadow of a flame on a wall. I see
the tanks, poling out their comic profiles. But then it's dim.
There was the place he walked to *in no uniform but the mind's fire.*
Then he turned from her, waving her back, waving away
the cheated, shouting executioners.

He kept touching himself, she said.
Over and over as if he was a newborn, discovering
his body. Then he began to bow,
                                        growing transparent.

                            My daughter lifts
toothpicks gingerly, one by one, from their chance
prop-up in the hotel ashtray, trying not to disturb
the stack's internal balance. Bored, she looks
where she sees us looking: sun touching the fragile

interdependent pile. *In no uniform but the mind's fire.*
What we are looking at took twenty years to imagine.
Then the pile collapses, as if sucked inward. It grows
dark outside as she begins to weep, the toothpicks
are realigned, gum snaps, *no red stars,* and he burns

                    before us, he goes on burning.

1

Onstage, the hero is arguing with his lover
of many years, a beautiful woman who has just
revealed to him that she is a man. Look closer!
She was born a man, but became perfect:

dependent on the soul's double-take. Unwound
like a chignon, shaken out like a plucked harp's
fan of gold: she's laughing, kneeling to pour tea.
She is too perfect, isn't she? each length of lacquered
nail clicking against mirrory surfaces that repeat
her made-up face wherever he looks for his own

        set expression. She recoils,
then releases herself abruptly in his senses
like a fragrant gasp of the atomizer. He can't even
see she is a spy. Intercepting state secrets
he willingly reveals
        late, over champagne, in bed, in the grip
of this committed self-caricature: love.
        He's a career diplomat, she is
                above nothing.

The plot: implausible but never exactly comic.
And a hero who is a fool, but such a scholar
of humiliation he begins to appear full of power,
        an object of awe.

Now he paints a Kabuki mask over his face,
lifts a dagger, as his Butterfly watches.
When he cuts his throat, the audience catches
                              its breath.

In his dressing-room, I wait out the curtain calls
leafing through a magazine: a wedding
in China where brides wear red. Her baby
face peeks, coquettish as sunrise between
                  the parted lips of a plum scroll.
When he bursts in,
a face sweating from his face, the audience's
cries still audible in the walls, he turns to me
so that I can see that he is empty: there is nothing left

not that anyone, even a wife, could name.

2

Now the hero wipes off his make-up
at the lighted mirror and he is you—the footlight mike,
still on, eavesdrops over the speakers: murmurs of the exiting.

Now the fat bossy dresser disappears (with an ironic bow to me)
to launder your kimono. You and I look at each other in the
                                        mirror,
                    one gaze exiting into the other.

                        Then people arrive. Champagne spills.
Later everyone troops, laughing, out the side exit
                        opening out onto Broadway

                    —which can only be reached by crossing
the empty dark stage still littered with fake white flowers.

                    I hang there looking out: silent perfect
                                                    rows,

pick up one of the blossoms Butterfly flung about so
carelessly in Act One.

                    She wanted him to see how, abandoned by him,
she was nothing—(the original opera readying her death!)
He turns away from her falling blossoms, but there's the eerie
    hope
she allows herself—born purely of acting—look closer,

born of her capacity to be . . . her own audience and
his? Separate melodramas, his inviolate. It's true. He once
loved her and look at the earth's gifts of empathy: Rain falls.

Sun rises. There is ritual. Look closer. If one learns mercy even
                                                    as theater,
          one comes to expect it.

There was the dream:
It traveled into us,
                like the intention
of an animal stalking us, or a god.
It came over us, a red shadow.
It did not move outward, like recognition.

You were afraid of how the body
scorned the figurative.
            How right that you feared
what resisted transformation: what I recover of it now

is relentless—bed, dark covers, lamplight,
flesh against flesh. And nothing can stop
the non-echo,
                the absence of repercussive sound
that makes the present deafening.

It will always be the present in that place.

If you could admit only this: there was no way
to wake from that dream. the rest of it, you see,
is my work: slowing the mind's quick progress

from the hypnotic of that startled world
to the empty solicitation of metaphor,
the loathsome poetic moment.
Crows, naturally, look at them gathering!

Consecutive murderous insights,
like our life stories, assembled from
little convenient logics, strategies,

slow death by interpretation.

UNSENT LETTER 2

You say you don't know who you are. I take
the plate of the homeless man and fill it
with macaroni and salad. Does he know who he is?
The next man comes up and I say "Would you
like a roll?" and he says "In the sand?" and laughs.

The next one is a woman, pregnant,
young. She asks in a small voice
if she can have some extra food.
We give her noodles, meat, greens.
She looks at her plate and begins

to cry. *I'm so tired,* she says
and stares into space, then at me.
I want to take her in my arms, but
I keep serving food, my hands in
the clear plastic gloves ice-cold

from the cold ocean wind. After a while
the pregnant girl has finished eating
with the others on the grass and wandered
away. I don't know who you are either.
We turned to each other,

                     once in blinding sunlight,
once in darkness. Going nowhere, in dream-quick
transit—as if we'd been abandoned
by our lives, freed of identity.

St. Augustine said to the crowd around the magus
that we do not understand miracles because we
do not understand the nature of time.

The magus collapsed duration: in his palm
the bean-pod unfurled into a shoot, flowered. I felt
your touch, not in time: in charmed space
where that seed accelerates, cycle by cycle.

And if we speed up transition—she'd have
another human being in her arms, an infant
—just like that—but she is homeless,
nothing to hold her outside her self.

He has left her, as we are all left. So we do not want
to hurry it, the miracle. It's better that it be served
in gradual sequence, do you see?—child, seducer, mother,
father, child, seducer . . . do you see? Faces: a food line, a *you,*

one frozen location of mercy: a final divided portion
                                        to set on each plate.

UNSENT LETTER 4

LAST TAKE

I watch them killing my husband.
        Trained assassins, pumping round after
round from behind a camouflage truck:
        they crouch toward his crippled form.

Under the white floodlights,
        blood jets sputter from his chest,
his head's thrown back. He shouts out a name, sliding down
        the white walls against the damp flag of his shadow.

A little guillotine shuts. Hands sponge the wall.
        He stands, alive again, so there's no
reason to fear this rehearsed fall, his captured cry,
        the badly cast revolution that asked his life.

The damask roses painted on the folding parlor screens
        of the phony embassy are real in a way, but the walls
are fake, and fake, too, the passion of these two naked
    human bodies
        embracing on the Aubusson: nevertheless, they obsess

the eye like any caress. Off-camera, the actor stroking his stubble
        of beard, the actress's hands on her own small breasts.
Presented with the mirror of our sentiments, it seems
        possible to believe that we love the world, ourselves—

Waiting in the wings like extras, full of desire
            projected away from us. These sky-high fingers
of light imply, offhand, all night, we stand in for God
            who is nothing to fear. He gets up and falls down again

in slow motion. A boom swings into the frame,
            then out. Loaded dice are shaken onto green felt before
the trembling hands of the unwitting victims. A roulette
            wheel turns: the red, the black, chemin de fer.

The train crosses the border: inside, rows of people jammed
            together, watch, weep. The real
sky behind the starry backdrop fills with stars. The lovers kiss.
            I want to ask How much? How much do we love each

other? But the director in his cherry-picker signals another take:
            The sky grows light. It's late.

BARRA DE NAVIDAD: ENVOI

—for my sister

Up the narrow road
from Barra de Navidad
they came, rippling
        in the heat:

    Women dressed as brides
children bearing blossoms,
their white skirts and veils
    blinding in the noon sun.

The cars stopped, one by one. Cold
inside our tinted glass interior
    I rolled my window down.

    Insubstantial as a mirage,
they hovered, pure white, improbable as the place:
a bleached spit of earth slid between the old half-
    alive volcano perched above us,
                    and the bay.

They had nothing to say.
Lifting pale crowns of hibiscus
from their hair, they shook free the heavy petals,
        then stood aside to reveal

the young man with an infant's white coffin
on his head. He strode forward
                intent.

The way a girl carries a water jug, one arm up,
in a perfect compromise of balance.
                              Undistracted

by our stares, he set his feet down against the white
bearings, the earth's sheer pall and compass—
              his gaze set far beyond us.

Still, I saw how if a single red blossom had fallen in his path,
he'd have stumbled—
                 into the shadow of the raptor circling above—
or into his wife's sudden keening,
spreading like blood unpent beneath the heat's surface.
So little remains in this feeble re-telling:
                 his regal stride
                 her single cumulative note . . .

                 grief following its image,
                 grief's true color vanishing:
                 snow on the sleeping volcano.

So it appears on our travels we've seen nothing new.
Though I notice how sounds gather daily to undermine the
    visible:
                 blue trees, amber beads, red bird's flight.

All of beauty's evasions,
then the mind's echo:

Dear Ellipsis,
Dear Night.

About the Author

Carol Muske (in fiction, Carol Muske Dukes) teaches at the University of Southern California in the Department of English. She is the author of five books of poetry and two novels. She is the recipient of many awards, including a John Simon Guggenheim Fellowship, a poetry fellowship from the NEA, an Ingram-Merrill grant, and the di Castagnola Prize from the Poetry Society of America, as well as several Pushcart Prizes. Her poems have been widely anthologized, appearing in *Best American Poetry*, *One Hundred Great Poems by Women*, *MotherSongs*, and many others. She is a regular reviewer for the *New York Times Book Review* and lives in Los Angeles with her husband, the actor David Dukes, and her daughter, Annie Cameron.